James Pearce

FOOD AND ITS FUNCTIONS

FOOD AND
ITS FUNCTIONS

SECOND EDITION

A. G. CAMERON
National College of Food Technology, Weybridge, Surrey

Illustrated by
A. G. STANDLEY

LONDON
EDWARD ARNOLD

© A. G. Cameron, 1968

First published 1964

Reprinted 1964, 1967

Second edition 1968

SBN: 7131 1541 6

Printed in Great Britain by
William Clowes and Sons, Limited, London and Beccles

Preface

I cannot synthesise a bun
By simply sitting in the sun.
                    J. B. S. Haldane

Man has taken hundreds of years to reach his present understanding of what food is and what our bodies need from food to keep us healthy. He has gradually unravelled much of the mystery of how plants build the nutrients that we need, how these nutrients in all their amazing complexity are constructed from simple building blocks. He has learnt how to cook and preserve food, how to increase food supplies and much else besides. He has not reached this understanding 'by simply sitting in the sun'; he has had to work very hard indeed. This book tells of some of his most important conclusions. In telling this story much has had to be left out, but I have tried to tell it simply and clearly, so that any young student with an elementary knowledge of general science will be able to understand it.

This book has been written for students in grammar and secondary modern schools. It should be particularly valuable to students studying Domestic Subjects for the General Certificate of Education 'O' level. It should also be useful as background reading for City and Guilds courses 150, 151, 243 and 244. Although the book contains much material covered in these courses, the contents have not been limited by considerations of any particular syllabus. The subject of Food and Nutrition is one that should surely be studied by every boy and girl and I have tried to write a book that will appeal to them—and which relates the subject to their everyday experience. I hope that in this way it may be found useful as a basis of courses in secondary modern schools where there may be no particular examination in view. In order that the subject matter may be integrated into a general course I have included a final chapter showing how the subject links up with other subjects such as history, geography, economics and current affairs.

There is a growing feeling to-day among progressive domestic science teachers that their subject should be taught from a scientific point of view; that the 'whys' and 'hows' of the subject are just as important as the practical skills. I believe that this scientific approach is most important, and I have emphasized it in what follows. In particular, Chapters 1 and 2 contain a very simple picture of how food is made

5

up of molecules, which in turn are built from atoms. It seems to me that it is only in this way that we can understand the importance of nutrients in terms of the units of which they are made. Such an approach leads on naturally to an account of digestion, where nutrients are seen to be broken down again into their constituent units.

In preparing this book I have had help from a number of sources. In particular I want to thank Mr. B. A. Fox, who has been associated with the book from its inception, and who has been largely responsible for Chapters 6 and 9. I should also like to pay tribute to the artist, Mr. Standley, for the excellence of his work. It is probably inevitable that in a book of this kind some inaccuracies will creep in, and I should be grateful if any such could be pointed out. Any suggestions for the improvement of the text will also be welcome.

A.G.C.

Preface to Second Edition

Three main objectives have been foremost in my mind in preparing this new edition. The first and most obvious one has been to eliminate errors, and the second has been to bring the book up to date. In some of the areas of knowledge covered by the book there have been important and spectacular advances in the last few years. For example, our understanding of the nature of proteins is growing rapidly and increasing numbers are being synthesized in the laboratory; also our knowledge of the internal structure of human cells has been drastically improved by the use of the electron microscope. These advances are considered briefly on pages 27 and 66 respectively.

The third and by far the most significant change in this edition relates to photographic material. Nearly 40 new photographs have been included and these have been chosen with several ends in view. For example, they have a much greater informational content than before and in many cases they extend the scope of the text; this is particularly true of the last chapter which has been completely reorganized. Another feature is the introduction of photographic sequences to describe commercial processes such as the making of bread, butter and cheese.

I would like to thank those who have written making suggestions for improving the text and it is to be hoped that the changes made will increase the usefulness and attractiveness of the book.

A.G.C.

Contents

Acknowledgments

We wish to thank the following for permission to reprint copyright photographs (page numbers in brackets): Almasy (177, 180); Barnaby's (cover); Birds Eye (159); British Egg Information Service (83); Dr P. N. Cardew (151); Domestos Ltd (161); Flour Advisory Bureau (56); W. J. Garnett (66); Alan Glanville/FAO (183); Kenya Coffee Industry (105); J. Lyons & Co Ltd (58); Medical Research Council and Drs J. C. Kendrew, H. C. Watson (27); NASA (187); National Milk Publicity Council (72); New Zealand Lamb Information Bureau (85); Odhams Ltd (25, 117, 123, 126, 144); H. E. C. Powers (18); Punch (175); Radio Times Hulton Picture Library (16, 107, 184); Rank Hovis McDougall (154); Shell (185); Smedley's Ltd (154, bottom); Studio Lisa Ltd (120); Tate & Lyle (63); John Topham (181); Unicef, Jack Ling (173); Unigate (51, 78, 83); Unilever Ltd (151); United Nations (16); Worthington Foods Inc (188, 189).

We should also like to thank the National Dairy Council for its permission to base Fig. 32 on material from charts published by the Council.

1 The Need for Food— and its Nature

THE BODY AS A LIVING MACHINE

In this book we shall be talking about food and about its connection with ourselves. In order to see why there is a connection between these two things, let us first of all think about what we mean by *life*. Life is very difficult to explain, but it is usually easy to recognize. Living things—whether animal or vegetable—have certain features in common. For instance, a young boy and a young apple tree are similar to each other in some ways. The most obvious likeness between them is that they are both growing. Also, they both need food and water and air if they are to keep on living, and this is true even when they have finished growing. Another very important feature about fully-grown living things is that they can reproduce themselves. The apples on an apple tree, for example, contain seeds from which new trees may develop. Similarly, a man produces sex cells which, when united with female sex cells, lead to the formation of new life. Human beings are like all other living things in that unless they are provided with a regular supply of food, water and air they die.

In some ways we can think of ourselves as living machines. A car engine works by using petrol as a fuel, and when the petrol and air are mixed and ignited inside the cylinder an explosion takes place that pushes the piston downwards and causes the car to move. In our case we use food as a fuel, and when food reacts with air inside our bodies, the reactions that take place enable us to live. These reactions keep us warm and enable us to move the various parts of our bodies. Fortunately for us the reaction between food and air is not exactly like that between petrol and air, for it would be alarming if explosions occurred inside us every time we ate a meal! In fact the reaction between food and air is a *slow* one and goes on all the time without our noticing it.

9

Before we can understand *why* we need food, we must take a closer look at our bodies. A solid framework of bone protects our more delicate parts and gives strength to the whole body structure. We call this framework the skeleton, and though it is strong it is also flexible so that we may move the various parts of our bodies easily. The skeleton acts as a shield for the system of organs inside us. At the hub of this system is the heart, which works an amazing transport system that reaches into every corner of our bodies, from the tops of our heads to the tips of our toes. The heart is a pump that makes blood flow round the body, and the blood takes food and oxygen to every part of the body and in exchange removes waste material. The main organs of the body are made from tissue material such as muscle tissue and nerve tissue. These tissues have their special jobs to do; muscle tissue for instance, is concerned with all body movement.

The body is a very complex machine with many different organs, each of which has its own task to perform. The lungs are concerned with supplying oxygen to the bloodstream and removing the waste gas carbon dioxide. Kidneys are concerned with removing liquid waste matter as urine. The brain is the main organ of the nervous system, being the principal controller of our actions and thinking. Each of these organs can only work if it is supplied with food, and this applies to all the other organs and tissues of the body which we have not mentioned. Let us now see what we need from food to keep all these organs and tissues working properly.

The Functions of Food

1. *Food for energy.* It is well known that 'You can't get something for nothing', and this idea may be applied to the use of energy by our bodies. Every time we move we use up energy; as we cannot get energy for nothing, it follows that we must replace it by some means or other. One of the functions of food is to replenish our store of energy.

When we move quickly we use up energy quickly; when we move slowly we use up energy more slowly. Even when we appear to be resting—as when we are asleep—we are using up energy simply because we are living. This is because the inside of the body is never at rest. Even when we *appear* to be resting the heart

10

must keep on beating and the lungs must keep on working, to mention only two organs. Both these processes involve movement and movement uses up energy. So simply to keep alive requires an additional supply. One of the things that food must do, therefore, is to supply us with energy.

2. *Food for body-building.* We have seen that growth, amongst other things, distinguishes living things from non-living. While we are young our bodies are developing; so during this time growth is very obvious. But even when we stop growing outwardly, our bodies continue to make new material. For instance, our hair and our nails keep on growing and when we cut or burn ourselves new skin is formed to replace the old. Indeed, skin and all our other tissues are continually being renewed. Remembering that we cannot get something for nothing, we realize that the material needed for growth and the renewal of our tissues must come from somewhere; as you will have guessed, it comes from food. Food then is needed for body-building—to enable us to grow, to repair and renew tissues and to create new life; that is to reproduce ourselves.

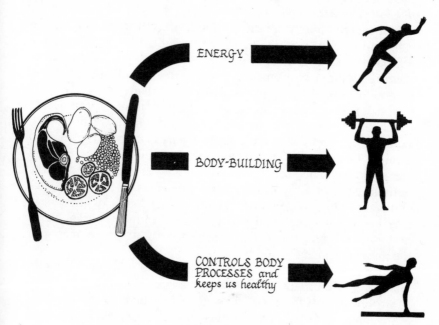

ENERGY

BODY-BUILDING

CONTROLS BODY PROCESSES and keeps us healthy

Fig. 1. What food does for us.

11

3. *Food for control of body processes.* Many processes are going on inside our bodies all the time and it is fairly obvious that if confusion is to be avoided, each process must be regulated so that it does not interfere with any other. The situation is rather like that at a busy road junction. If the traffic is to be kept moving without any collisions taking place, some form of control—a policeman or traffic lights—is needed. Inside our bodies it is food that is used to control our body processes and keep us healthy.

Nutrients and Nutrition

We cannot live by eating anything that we choose. For example, it is impossible to live by eating nothing but cream cakes. We must choose what we eat—that is our *diet*—with care, so that it keeps us healthy. It will only do this if it carries out the three jobs mentioned above. And it can only do this if it contains substances called *nutrients*. Although there are hundreds of different foods there are only a few types of nutrients. In fact there are only six types and these are: *carbohydrates, fats, proteins, mineral elements, water* and *vitamins.* & *roughage*

Not everything that we eat is a food. A substance can only be called food if it contains at least one nutrient. Thus sugar is a food because it is a carbohydrate. Salt also is a food because it consists of mineral elements. Pepper, on the other hand, is not a food because it does not contain a nutrient; it merely adds flavour to other foods. Sometimes it is not at all easy to decide which of the things we eat are foods and which are not. For example, tea and coffee are usually a part of our daily diet, and it might be presumed that they would be foods. However, they are not; they only contain minute traces of nutrients and the nutrient value of a cup of tea or coffee depends on the milk, sugar and water which it contains. On the other hand, unlikely as it may seem, rusty pots and cutlery have a certain nutrient value because they are sources of iron, which is a nutrient belonging to the mineral element group.

In contrast to those foods, such as sugar and salt, which contain one type of nutrient there are others which contain several. Most foods are of this kind and some very valuable foods, such as milk, contain a variety of nutrients and can carry out all three of the jobs that food must do.

12

Much of what follows will be concerned either with the nutrients which are found in various foods or with the effect that these nutrients have on our bodies. The study of these effects is called *nutrition*. For example, if our diet is well chosen we shall not only get a supply of all six nutrients, but we shall get them in the right proportions for our bodies' needs. In such cases our bodies receive all that they need to remain healthy and we enjoy good nutrition. On the other hand, if our diet gives us too little of the nutrients we need our health suffers and we are said to be in a state of *under-nutrition*. If our diet continues to give us a smaller and smaller supply of nutrients we eventually starve (see page 16).

Each nutrient carries out at least one of the three tasks of food, and some nutrients are able to do more than one job. Whereas fat, for example, only supplies us with energy, other nutrients, such as mineral elements and vitamins, both control body processes and are concerned with growth and repair. The jobs that the various nutrients do is shown in Fig. 2. Important foods which provide these nutrients are also shown. Thus starchy foods, such as bread and potatoes, and sugary foods, such as jam and honey, are good sources of carbohydrate. Body-building proteins are found particularly in such foods as meat, fish, eggs and cheese, while butter, margarine and lard are important sources of fat.

What Food is Made of

When we pick up a piece of coal we may wonder what it contains. Coal is mainly *carbon*, and carbon is an example of an *element*, which means that it is a simple kind of material which cannot be split up into anything simpler. If we start hammering a piece of coal, we shall split it up into smaller and smaller pieces until we have ground it into a fine dust. But it will still be mainly carbon. Let us now imagine that a speck of carbon was broken down into even smaller pieces. Soon the speck would become invisible and eventually it would become so small that it would be impossible to split it any further. We would then have the smallest piece of carbon that could exist. Such a particle is called an *atom*.

Every element is made up of atoms which means that everything we know—whether solid, liquid or gas—is atomic. All the atoms of an element are alike, but they differ in size from the atoms of every other element. It is very difficult to imagine the size of atoms because they are so very small. An illustration may

Fig. 2. The nutrients—showing *some* important foods in which they are found and also their tasks in the body.

perhaps make this clearer. The smallest atoms are those of the gas *hydrogen*. If we were to take a hollow pin's head and fill it with hydrogen, we should have enough hydrogen atoms to give several *million* to each person living on the earth.

Although we know of about one hundred elements, only a dozen or so of these are important in foods. These elements are listed in the table below, together with a brief description of what they are like. The elements which are most often found in foods are at the top of the table.

Elements of importance in Foods

Name of element	Description of element
Carbon	Black solid
Hydrogen	Lightest gas known
Oxygen	Colourless gas
Nitrogen	Colourless gas
Sulphur	Yellow solid
Sodium	Soft silvery metal
Calcium	Silvery metal
Potassium	Soft silvery metal
Chlorine	Yellow poisonous gas
Phosphorus	Red solid
Iron	Greyish metal
Iodine	Violet solid
Fluorine	Yellowish gas

Atoms rarely exist on their own. They normally link up in groups of two or more, and such a group is called a *molecule*.

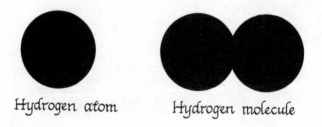

Hydrogen atom   Hydrogen molecule

Fig. 3.

15

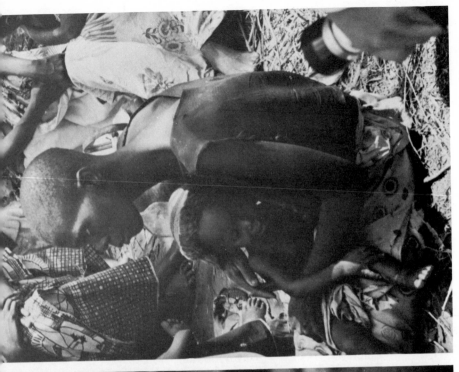

A poor diet produces under-nutrition and health suffers.

A well chosen diet gives good nutrition and helps us to remain

Thus hydrogen gas is made up of molecules of hydrogen, and each molecule consists of two atoms. (Fig. 3.)

When atoms of different elements join together they form a *compound*. For example, water is a simple compound and one water molecule consists of two atoms of hydrogen linked to one atom of oyxgen.

Fig. 4.

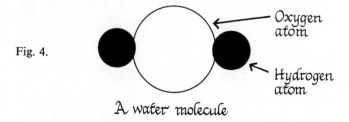

Oxygen atom

Hydrogen atom

A water molecule

It may seem surprising that some of the elements found in food are poisonous gases or metallic solids. The explanation of this is that these elements never occur free in foods, but are in the form of compounds—and compounds have quite different properties from the elements of which they are made. Thus water is a colourless liquid, though it is made up of two elements which are both gases. When an atom of the metal sodium becomes joined to an atom of the poisonous gas chlorine a molecule of sodium chloride or salt is formed. As we have already noted, this is a food and has no similarity to the elements from which it is made.

Although only a few elements commonly occur in food, they can join together in a very large number of ways, so that many different compounds are found in foods. For example, all carbohydrates, all oils and fats and some vitamins are made up of the three elements carbon, hydrogen and oxygen. If we add two more elements—nitrogen and sulphur—we can also include most proteins. Considering proteins alone we find, probably to our surprise, that thousands of different proteins are found in foods.

The simplest molecules that occur in food—such as water and sodium chloride—are made up of only two or three atoms, and these molecules are very small indeed. Their smallness can be imagined more easily if we use an illustration. If we could take one drop of water and magnify it until it was the size of the earth, a water molecule would only be about the size of a small apple.

Most of the compounds found in food are more complicated than water and salt. The simplest type of carbohydrate, such as

17

glucose, contains 24 atoms in its molecule—6 atoms of carbon, 6 of oxygen and 12 of hydrogen. Fats are rather larger and a typical fat molecule contains about 170 atoms. Some molecules

Molecules are very small indeed; each of these magnified sugar crystals contains millions upon millions of sugar molecules.

found in food contain a very large number of atoms indeed. Proteins, for example, are very complex and a large protein molecule will contain several hundred thousand atoms. However, even such large molecules are very small indeed by normal standards, and are far too small to be seen by even the best microscope.

SUMMARY

Our bodies are living machines which can only live if they are supplied with food, water and air. Our body system needs food for three reasons. It needs food to supply energy for movement and internal processes, to provide material for the growth and repair of tissues and to control the other processes. Our diet is able to carry out these tasks because it contains six types of nutrients—carbohydrates, fats, proteins, mineral elements, water and vitamins. No substance can be called a food unless it contains at least one type of nutrient. Each nutrient is made up of two or more elements and the elements are composed of atoms. The elements in food are present in the form of compounds, and though food is made up of only about twelve elements, thousands of different food compounds are known.

2 The Nature of Nutrients

In this chapter we are going to study the structure of the nutrients more closely. We have already discussed the structure of water and seen how each molecule is made up of two atoms of hydrogen and one atom of oxygen. We do not need to say any more about water here, except that though we do not usually refer to water as a food, it is nevertheless a nutrient. Water is a part of nearly all foods and many foods, such as fruit and leafy vegetables, are nearly all water. Even so-called 'dry' foods, such as bread, are about one-third water.

CARBOHYDRATES

We are like other animals in that we cannot make carbohydrates for ourselves. Luckily for us, plants have the power to build up or *synthesize* carbohydrates. Therefore, in order to get the carbohydrates that our bodies need, we can use plants—or animals that have fed on plants—as food.

Plants build up carbohydrates from very simple starting materials. In fact all they need is the gas carbon dioxide, water and sunlight. As carbohydrates are energy-providing substances they must contain a store of energy. This stored energy is obtained from sunlight when carbohydrate is made out of carbon dioxide and water. This process is called *photosynthesis*, which means 'put together by light', and it occurs in the green leaves of the plant.

At first photosynthesis leads to the formation of simple sugars, such as *glucose*. Carbon dioxide contains carbon and oxygen linked together. Therefore, when carbon dioxide combines with water, a substance containing carbon, hydrogen and oxygen is formed. All carbohydrates are made up of these three elements,

19

and in the simple case of glucose each molecule is small. In later stages of photosynthesis larger carbohydrate molecules are built up. The end product of this process is *starch*, which is the form in which plants store energy for future use.

Simple Sugars

Glucose is an example of a *simple sugar* or *monosaccharide*. It is found in grapes and other sweet fruits and also in honey. Other examples are *fructose*, which occurs with glucose in sweet fruits and honey, and *galactose*, which is not found in food. Both fructose and galactose contain the same number of carbon, hydrogen and oxygen atoms as glucose. The only difference between them is the way in which the atoms are arranged in the molecule. Molecules of glucose, fructose and galactose are shown in Fig. 5.

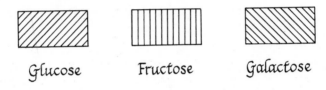

Fig. 5.

They have all been given the same shape to indicate that they are similar, but they have been shaded differently to indicate that they are not exactly the same. It will be understood that here, and elsewhere in the book, the shapes given to molecules are not their actual shapes; the shapes in the diagrams are chosen merely to help you to understand the way molecules are built up or changed in reactions.

Glucose, fructose and galactose all have similar properties. They are all white, crystalline solids and they are all sweet. They dissolve easily in water to form colourless, sweet solutions.

Double Sugars

Double sugars or *disaccharides* are built up from two simple sugar molecules. The most familiar double sugar is ordinary

household sugar or *sucrose*. Sucrose is built up from one molecule of glucose and one molecule of fructose and that, of course,
is why it is called a *double* sugar (Fig. 6).

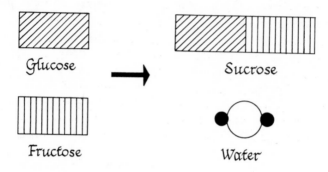

Fig. 6. The formation of sucrose and water from glucose and fructose.

There are two other important double sugars. One is *lactose*
or *milk sugar*, which is built up from one molecule of glucose and
one of galactose. As its name suggests, milk sugar is found in the
milk of animals. The other important double sugar is *maltose* or
malt sugar, which is built up from two molecules of glucose.

Double sugars are white, sweet crystalline solids and they dissolve in water to give clear, colourless solutions.

Sucrose is by far the most important sugar in our diet; in Great
Britain we consume roughly two pounds per person per week.

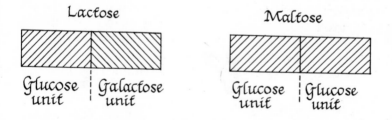

Fig. 7. The structure of lactose and maltose, showing how they are built up
from two simple sugar units.

It has a very important property which we shall now consider. It we warm a solution of sucrose in water, to which a little acid has been added, we find that the sucrose is broken down into the simple sugars glucose and fructose from which it was built. This splitting of the sucrose molecule is brought about by the water, though the acid which is present helps to speed up the reaction. Such a splitting by water is called a *hydrolysis*. You can picture it as shown in Fig. 8.

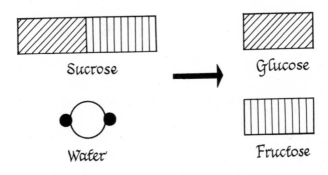

Fig. 8. The hydrolysis of sucrose into glucose and fructose.

If you look carefully at this reaction you will notice that it is the reverse of what happened when a sucrose molecule was built up from glucose and fructose as shown in Fig. 6. This suggests that the build-up of sucrose is not simply the linking together of glucose and fructose. It is a reaction which involves the splitting out of one molecule of water. We shall see in what follows that water has a most important role to play in very many of the processes concerned both in the build-up of foods in plants and in their later break-down in man and animals.

The mixture of glucose and fructose formed by hydrolysing sugar is called *invert-sugar*. Honey—which is made by bees—is mainly invert-sugar together with about one-fifth water and small amounts of flavouring. Bees collect nectar—which is mainly sucrose—from flowers, and as the sucrose passes through the bee it is converted by hydrolysis into invert-sugar. The special flavour

22

of honey depends upon the flavourings in the flowers from which the bees collect their nectar. For instance, if you have ever tasted heather honey and clover honey you will have noticed that each has a distinctive flavour of its own. This is due to the different flavouring substances found in heather and clover flowers. Long ago, before man had discovered the secret of how to get sugar from sugar beet or sugar cane, honey was an important part of the diet, being the only sweetening agent known.

When sucrose is hydrolysed into invert-sugar the process is known as *inversion*, and it is often an important process in food-making. Thus in making jam, fruit is boiled with sucrose solution, and in the presence of acids contained in the fruit, inversion occurs (see page 25). This is of great importance because invert-sugar prevents jam from crystallizing when it is stored. Invert-sugar must also be present in boiled sweets and toffee to prevent the crystallization that would otherwise occur. Crystallization is undesirable because it makes sweets gritty and 'sugary'. Fruit drinks, made from fresh fruit and sucrose, also contain invert-sugar; you will be able to work out why for yourself.

Polysaccharides

The main examples of polysaccharides (meaning *many sugars*) found in food are *starch* and *cellulose*. Like the simple sugars, polysaccharides are built up from simple materials in plants by photosynthesis. Although polysaccharide molecules are very much bigger than those of simple sugars, it is fairly easy to understand their construction because they are built from monosaccharide units, just like disaccharides.

Starch is made up of glucose units, which are linked together as indicated in Fig. 9. The diagram shows only a very small part of

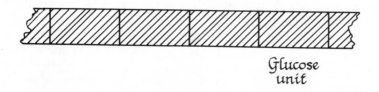

Glucose
unit

Fig. 9. A small part of a starch molecule, showing four glucose units.

a starch molecule because a complete molecule contains many thousands of linked glucose units, which could not possibly all be shown in a single diagram. The starch molecule is rather like a long string of similar beads which are strung end to end.

Starch is stored by plants as a reserve supply of energy. It is found stored in the stems of plants as in the sago palm, in the tubers as in potatoes and in the roots as in cassava, from which tapioca is made. It is also found in seeds, such as the cereal grains —wheat, barley and oats—and in unripe fruit.

As more and more glucose units are joined together—each linkage involving the splitting out of one water molecule—the sugar-like properties are lost. Thus starch, which is a white solid, differs from the sugars in that it is not sweet and that it will not dissolve in cold water. If you look at starch through a microscope you will find that it is made up of tiny grains or granules. The shape and size of the grains depend upon the plant from which they have come.

The polysaccharide *pectin* has no direct value as a food, but is valuable as a setting agent in jam-making. Certain fruit, such as apples, plums and citrus fruit are rich in pectin, and so jam made from such fruit sets easily. The pectin is extracted by simmering the fruit (in water for such fruit as plums and damsons) for a period before sugar is added. Fruit containing little pectin— such as strawberries and marrow—are difficult to make into jam, and additional pectin or pectin-rich fruit may be added to promote setting.

Cellulose—like starch—is built up from large numbers of glucose units which become linked together through the splitting out of water molecules. The properties of cellulose are quite different from those of starch, however, because the linking process takes place in a slightly different way. Cellulose is found in fruits and vegetables, where it strengthens the walls of the plant; also in the husks of wheat and other cereal grains. Indeed, all forms of plant life—from the toughest tree-trunk to the softest cotton wool —contain cellulose.

Cellulose, like starch, has lost the sugar-like properties of glucose. It forms hair-like fibres which are not sweet and will not dissolve in water. You might expect that it would be possible to break down or hydrolyse cellulose into glucose molecules, just as it was possible to hydrolyse sucrose into the units from which it was built. Although it is possible to do this, it is much more

Making strawberry jam, showing the addition of lemon juice to the strawberries (top) and the bottling of the jam (bottom). Strawberries contain little acid so that an acid fruit juice is added to promote inversion.

difficult to carry out than was the case with sucrose and, as we shall see in the next chapter, this has an important consequence in digestion.

PROTEINS

We have seen that because animals cannot make their own carbohydrate they must obtain it from their food. In a similar way animals, including man, cannot make their own protein and so they have to obtain their protein needs from plants, which can make their own protein out of simple starting materials. Alternatively they can obtain their protein by eating animals which have themselves fed on plants.

In addition to the elements carbon, hydrogen and oxygen that are present in carbohydrates, proteins always contain nitrogen, often sulphur and sometimes phosphorus. Proteins are very complicated substances, but we can easily get some idea of their structure because they are built up from large numbers of fairly simple units called *amino acids*. A single protein molecule of average size will contain as many as 500 amino acid units.

Figure 10 shows the way in which amino acids link together to form a long-chain protein molecule. Every time that two amino

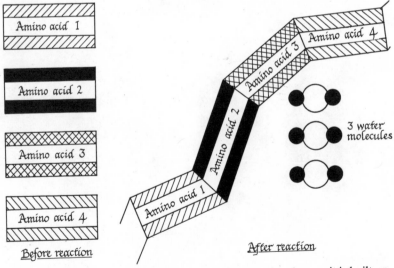

Fig. 10. A small portion of a protein molecule, showing the way it is built up from amino acids.

acids join up a molecule of water is split out.   This will remind
you of what happened when glucose and fructose joined together
to form sucrose, and it is indeed a similar sort of reaction.   Do not
think, however, that you know all about the structure of proteins
because you know that they are made of long chains of linked
amino acids.   The chains of amino acids are not in simple
straight lines, but are zig-zag shaped, coiled and linked to other
chains in a variety of ways.

The problem of trying to work out exactly what proteins are
like is a very difficult one and scientists in different parts of the
world have been trying to solve it for many years.   Recently there
has been exciting progress in this field, and we now know the complete structure of several proteins such as the one shown below.

A model of a protein molecule; each ball represents an atom.

This model will give you some idea of the complexity of proteins and you can see the way in which the many thousands of atoms are linked together.

If you compare Fig. 10 with Fig. 9, which shows part of a starch molecule, you will notice an important difference. Whereas a starch molecule contains the *same* unit repeated over and over again, a protein molecule contains a number of *different* units.

About twenty different amino acids are found in protein foods. This may not seem a very large number, but it means that there are a great many different ways in which they may be arranged. This can be appreciated if you remember that a protein molecule may contain 500 linked amino acids. With 20 *different* amino acids to choose from, almost endless arrangements are possible. In fact the number is so very large—more than a million, million, million —that it cannot be imagined!

Not all the 20 amino acids found in food proteins are present in any one protein, and this cuts down the number of possible arrangements. Even so you will see why thousands of different food proteins exist. Luckily for us we need not remember the names of all these different proteins, because the important thing about a protein is the amino acids that it contains (see page 34).

Only the simplest proteins consist entirely of amino acids. Other proteins, called *conjugated* proteins, contain other types of unit in their molecule. For example, the protein *casein*, which is the main protein found in milk and cheese, contains a phosphorus compound linked to the amino acid units.

To get some idea of the properties of proteins, let us take as an example a simple protein containing nothing but amino acids. *Ovalbumin*, found in egg white, is such a protein. This substance is soluble in water, and egg white is little more than a very weak solution of ovalbumin in water. If you take a little egg white and start to heat it, you will notice that its appearance starts to change. A little above 60°C. the egg white starts to become solid. If you continue to heat, you will notice that all the egg white turns into a soft white solid; this becomes harder on further heating. This is what happens, of course, when you boil an egg. The effect of heat on proteins is called *coagulation*.

Proteins are very delicate substances and tend to suffer a change in properties very easily. For instance, if you beat up egg white it becomes foamy, and if you beat it long enough, the foam becomes quite stiff. This is because the ovalbumin has been partly

coagulated.   If the foam is heated, further coagulation occurs, and the foam becomes rigid.   This is what happens in the making of meringues.

OILS AND FATS

Fats, such as butter and margarine, are familiar to us all.   We recognise them at once by their appearance and smell, their greasy feel and taste and their insolubility in water.   They contain the same three elements as carbohydrates, namely carbon, hydrogen and oyxgen.   Fat molecules are much smaller than those of carbohydrates, and they are always built from the same number of units. A molecule of fat contains four linked units, one unit being of a different *kind* from the other three.

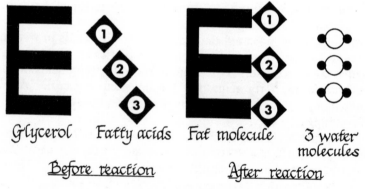

Glycerol Fatty acids Fat molecule 3 water molecules

Before reaction After reaction

Fig. 11.   Formation of a fat molecule.

All food fats are built up from a substance called *glycerine* or *glycerol*.   This is a sweet and rather syrupy colourless liquid.   It is able to link up with three other molecules, and this is the reason why fats always contain four units.   The other type of molecule involved is an *acid*.   You will be familiar with acidic substances such as vinegar and lemon juice.   Acids are noted for their sourness and their ability to change the colour of some dyes.   For example, they change the colour of litmus from blue to red.   The acids which react with glycerol to form fats are called *fatty acids*. The way in which the four molecules link together is pictured in Fig. 11.   Each time a fatty acid molecule becomes linked to a glycerol molecule, a molecule of water is split out, so that three

29

molecules of water are produced for each molecule of fat. A number of different fatty acids combine with glycerol to form fats. Among the most important are *palmitic acid* and *stearic acid*, which are found in most fats.

We have not yet said anything about oils. The most obvious difference between oils and fats is that oils are liquids at normal air temperatures, whereas fats are solids at such temperatures. Oils are constructed from glycerol and fatty acids in the same way as fats. The reason why they normally occur as liquids is that they contain a large proportion of a type of fatty acid known as an *unsaturated* fatty acid. The best known example of such an acid is *oleic acid*, which occurs to some extent in all natural oils and fats, but particularly in some oils, such as olive oil. Hard fats, such as margarine, contain only a small proportion of unsaturated fatty acids, while soft fats, such as lard, contain a higher proportion of unsaturated fatty acids, and oils, such as olive oil, contain a still higher proportion.

It must be emphasized that there are no *free* acids in pure oils and fats. Fats have quite different properties from the acids of which they are made. When one refers to the fatty acids in a fat, one means the fatty acids that are linked to glycerol. As was shown in the last chapter when molecules combine their properties are completely altered.

Pure fats are white solids and pure oils are colourless liquids. Both oils and fats are insoluble in water. You can test this for yourself by adding a little olive (or other) oil to water. The oil and the water form two separate layers, and on shaking they still remain separate, with small drops of oil spread through the water. On standing the two layers reform, showing that the oil has not dissolved in the water.

Oils and fats are much more stable to heat than proteins. They can be heated to a temperature (Centigrade) two, or even three, times as great as that of boiling water before any change occurs. For this reason, food which is best cooked at a high temperature, is often fried in hot fat rather than being boiled in water.

VITAMINS

You will have noticed that carbohydrates, proteins and fats are each constructed according to a definite pattern. All fats, for example, are built up in the same way from fatty acids and glycerol.

Members of the vitamin group, however, are not built up according to a common plan. Each vitamin is built up in a different way. They all contain the three elements carbon, hydrogen and oxygen, most contain nitrogen, and occasionally elements such as sulphur and phosphorus occur.

You may think it rather strange that we should put vitamins together into a single group, when they are really so different from each other. The reason for this is very simple. When vitamins were discovered nothing was known about how they were built. Until early in this century it was believed that a diet containing adequate amounts of carbohydrates, proteins, fats, mineral elements and water would be sufficient for the maintenance of health. When such an artificial diet was tried out, however, it was found that it did not maintain health. The name of vitamin was therefore given to the group of substances which, when added in small amounts to the diet mentioned above, enabled it to maintain health. We shall deal fully with vitamins in Chapter 6.

MINERAL ELEMENTS

You are probably familiar with minerals, such as limestone and rock salt, that are dug out of the earth. You may be rather puzzled, however, to see any connection between them and the food that we eat. In fact the term mineral element is not a very good one to describe a group of nutrients because, for instance, we obviously cannot eat metals which form a part of natural minerals. The clue to the puzzle may be found in the last chapter. Though we cannot eat the mineral element sodium, we can eat sodium chloride, formed when sodium combines with chlorine. This is because the compound sodium chloride is quite unlike the sodium and chlorine from which it is made. In other words, while it is true to say that we must obtain mineral elements from our diet, it is not true to say that we eat the elements themselves. What we actually eat are the compounds which have been built from mineral elements. Thus by eating salt we obtain the mineral elements, sodium and chlorine. We could even eat limestone—though it would not be very pleasant—and obtain another mineral element that we need, namely calcium. Indeed nowadays chalk, which is powdered limestone, is added to nearly all the flour from which our bread is made. This is done to ensure that we do not go short of calcium.

31

Other examples of mineral elements that we must obtain from our food are *phosphorus, iron* and *iodine*. Although we need only small amounts of the last two, we could not live without them.

In addition to the mineral elements mentioned above, we need very tiny amounts of a number of others. The amounts that we need are so small—mere traces—that we call them *trace elements*. Though we need only such small amounts, we can no more do without trace elements than we can do without those, such as calcium, which we need in relatively large amounts. Iodine is a trace element and other examples are *manganese, zinc, cobalt* and *copper*. Since these elements are needed in such small amounts, we need not bother about which foods contain them. Almost any diet will supply us with more of these elements than we need.

SUMMARY

Carbohydrates are divided into simple sugars (monosaccharides), double sugars (disaccharides) built from two simple sugar units, and polysaccharides built from many simple sugar units. Man is unable to make his own carbohydrate, and obtains his supplies from plants which make their own carbohydate by photosynthesis. The most important double sugar is sucrose, built from one molecule of glucose and one molecule of fructose. It can be broken down again into these simple sugars by hydrolysis, the process being called inversion and the sugar mixture produced invert sugar. Inversion is important in making jam, boiled sweets and toffee. The most important polysaccharides are starch and cellulose, both of which are built from many glucose units.

Protein molecules are made up of large numbers of amino acid units joined together to form complex chains. They are delicate substances and soluble proteins coagulate when heated, and even to some extent when shaken. Fat molecules are small compared to those of proteins, being built from one molecule of glycerol and three fatty acid molecules. Oils are similar to fats except that they contain a greater proportion of unsaturated fatty acids.

The different vitamins are not constructed on a common plan. They are put together as a group because without any one of them, a diet containing all the other types of nutrient cannot maintain health. Mineral elements are eaten in the form of salts. We need some mineral elements, such as calcium, in fairly large amounts; others, such as iodine and copper, are only needed in tiny quantities.

3 Digestion

It's a very odd thing,
As odd as can be,
That whatever Miss T. eats,
Turns into Miss T.

De la Mare

It is indeed a very odd thing—a very remarkable thing—that no matter what we eat, the structure of our bodies changes very little. There is little obvious similarity between the nature of the food we eat and the nature of our bodies. Indeed, the difference between them is so great that most of the food we eat is of no use to us at all until its nature has been completely changed. The process by which the nature of food is changed in the body is called *digestion*.

Many of the molecules found in food are very large as molecules go. You may remember, for example, that a large protein molecule may contain several hundred thousand atoms. Such molecules are far too large to be of use to the body. Before they can be used they must be broken down into molecules which are small enough to be *absorbed* into the bloodstream. After digestion food is absorbed into the blood in rather the same way that water is absorbed into a sponge. We can sum the matter up by saying that most of the nutrients of food cannot be used by our bodies until they have been digested and absorbed.

Let us begin by considering carbohydrates. One of the commonest forms of carbohydrate in food is starch. A starch molecule is large, being built up from a large number of glucose units. It is of no use to our bodies until it has been broken down into small soluble units that can be absorbed. This breakdown process occurs in stages; the starch molecule is broken down bit by bit until a molecule containing only two glucose units is left. This substance is maltose as we saw on page 21. However the body cannot use even this small molecule until it has been broken in half to form two glucose molecules. The result of this step-by-step

33

breakdown process is that starch is completely converted into glucose.

We must next think of how this breakdown process occurs. It is fairly obvious that carbohydrate molecules do not simply fall apart when they are eaten, because the glucose units are firmly linked together. Some agent is needed to break the links between the glucose units. We shall get a clue to what happens from Fig. 8 on page 22, where the breakdown of sucrose is shown as being brought about by water, i.e. it is a hydrolysis. A solution of starch in water can also be hydrolysed and this may be done by boiling it with a little acid for a few minutes. After the water has broken all the links between the glucose units, we are left with a solution of glucose. The digestion of sucrose and starch in the body also takes place by hydrolysis.

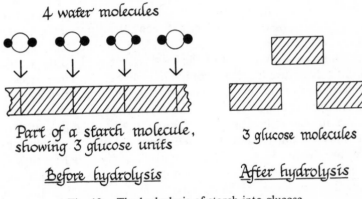

Fig. 12. The hydrolysis of starch into glucose.

Just as starch molecules must be broken down into glucose molecules before they can be used by our bodies, so proteins must be broken down into amino acids. As we have seen, protein molecules consist of linked amino acid units, and in digestion the links which join the amino acid units are broken down step by step until each protein molecule has been completely converted into the amino acids from which it was built. The breakage of the links between amino acid units is brought about by hydrolysis.

Fats also are hydrolysed during digestion. Hydrolysis again takes place in stages, one fatty acid molecule being removed from a fat molecule in each stage. A fat molecule is sometimes called a *triglyceride*, because *three* fatty acid molecules become joined to

one *glycerol* molecule to form it. When one fatty acid molecule is split off from a fat molecule, the resulting molecule is called a *diglyceride* and if a further fatty acid molecule is removed a *monoglyceride* is formed. During digestion both monoglycerides and diglycerides are produced. The final stage, in which a monoglyceride is hydrolysed to glycerol, does not take place to any large extent. The first stage in the hydrolysis is shown in Fig. 13.

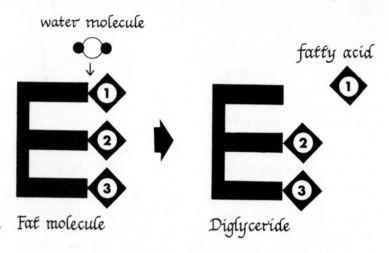

Fig. 13.   The first stage in the hydrolysis of a fat molecule.

Enzymes and Digestion

We have seen that during digestion carbohydrates, proteins and fats are broken down into simple molecules by hydrolysis. We have also seen that hydrolysis cannot take place without water. But water itself is not enough. We cannot hydrolyse sucrose simply by making a solution of it in water; we must also add an acid. In the same way water alone is not enough to bring about hydrolysis in our bodies. In the stomach acid helps to bring about hydrolysis, but the main hydrolysing agents in the body are most important substances called *enzymes*.

Enzymes are proteins. Thousands of different enzymes are known, and they are all constructed out of large numbers of connected amino acid units. They are of vital importance in all the reactions going on in our bodies. Enzymes which assist digestive processes are all involved in hydrolysis and so they are

called *hydrolysing enzymes.* Later in the book we shall meet other types of enzymes which assist other sorts of reactions.

Only a small quantity of a hydrolysing enzyme is needed to bring about the hydrolysis of a large amount of food. This is because although enzymes speed up hydrolysis, they are not used up in the process. Such substances are called *catalysts.* A catalyst may be likened to a moving escalator. If you climb an escalator that is not moving, it is a slow business. When the escalator is moving upwards, however, you can climb much more quickly, and when you step off at the top, the part you were standing on moves round again to the bottom. It is then available to carry someone else to the top. It is obvious that if you want to carry a large number of people up a stair quickly—as happens in the rush-hour on the London Underground—it is much better to use a moving escalator than a fixed stair.

There are two points to notice about an escalator. The first is that you use only the surface of the escalator, and the second is that after you have used the escalator it is still available for the use of other people. The catalytic action of an enzyme is rather similar. The enzyme acts by making its surface available to other substances, and for this reason it is called a *surface catalyst.*

In hydrolysis water reacts with some other substance, which we can call substance A. Before they can react, water and substance A must come together, and the enzyme surface is available to enable this to occur. If a molecule of substance A contains two units B and C linked together, hydrolysis breaks the link, so producing B and C as separate molecules. If substance A is sucrose, for example, B and C are glucose and fructose. After the new molecules have been formed, they move away from the enzyme surface, which is then ready to receive more molecules. In this way the enzyme surface can be used again and again, so that very little enzyme is needed to bring about the hydrolysis of a large number of molecules of A. This process is pictured in Fig. 14.

There is one way in which the action of an enzyme is quite different from that of an escalator. The escalator surface can be used by anyone, but an enzyme surface is so shaped that often it can be used by water and only *one* other substance. The reason for this will be clear from Fig. 14. Molecule A exactly fits the shape of the enzyme surface. You can compare enzyme hydrolysis to the fit of a key into a lock, with A acting as the key, and

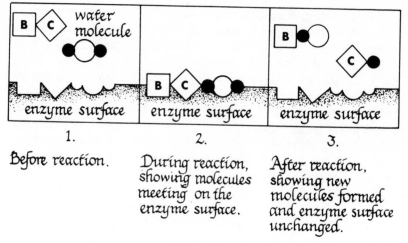

1.

Before reaction.

2.

During reaction, showing molecules meeting on the enzyme surface.

3.

After reaction, showing new molecules formed and enzyme surface unchanged.

Fig. 14. How an enzyme catalyses hydrolysis.

the enzyme as the lock.   Only when the molecules of a substance fit into the enzyme surface can the enzyme act as a catalyst.   The enzyme *lactase*, for example, acts as a catalyst to the sugar *lactose*, but it does not act as a catalyst to any other substance.   This is like having a burglar-proof lock, which can only be opened by one particular key.

The names of enzymes usually end in *-ase*.   Thus the hydrolysis of *maltose* is catalysed by *maltase*, just as that of lact*ose* is catalysed by lact*ase*.

As each enzyme will only catalyse the hydrolysis of one particular substance—or of a group of substances which have molecules of a similar shape—a very large number of enzymes is needed for the digestion of food.   We shall now consider in greater detail the stages of digestion in the body but, because so many enzymes are involved, we shall only be able to refer to a few of them by name.

Stages of Digestion

The digestive system is really a very long tube—about thirty feet long in an adult—which is open at both ends.   Food enters at the mouth, and passes slowly through the system being digested and absorbed on the way.   Any food that is left is removed as waste from the other end of the tube, which is called the anus.   The main parts of the digestive system are shown in Fig. 15.

Digestion begins as soon as food is eaten. The action of chewing food with our teeth breaks it into smaller pieces. These smaller pieces become mixed with a watery substance called *saliva*, which is produced by the *salivary glands*. Saliva moistens the food and makes it easier to swallow. It also contains a starch-splitting enzyme or amylase, which helps in the first stage of breaking down cooked starchy food. (*Amylase* is the general name given to any enzyme concerned with hydrolysing starchy foods.) The sight of a well-cooked meal, an appetizing smell or even the thought of a good meal aid digestion because they cause the salivary glands to produce plenty of saliva.

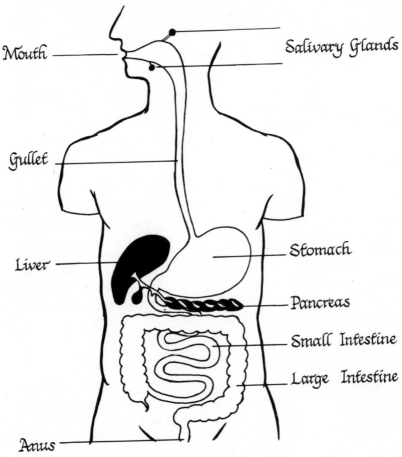

Fig. 15. The digestive system.

Food passes from the mouth into the gullet and is carried down the gullet and into the stomach by gentle muscular action. Muscular action continues in the stomach and this causes food to become mixed with *gastric juice*, which is poured forth from the lining of the stomach. The appearance, smell and flavour of good food all help in ensuring a good flow of gastric juice. Gastric juice is an acidic watery liquid, which contains hydrochloric acid and a number of enzymes. The chief enzyme is *pepsin*, which catalyses the hydrolysis of proteins. Pepsin cannot assist in breaking all the links joining the amino acids in a protein molecule; indeed it can only break a few links, so in the stomach proteins are not broken down very much.

You will notice that not much digestion takes place in the stomach. The main purpose of the stomach is to prepare food for the main stage of digestion which takes place in the *small intestine*. This is a very long, narrow and coiled tube. As soon as food passes from the stomach into the upper part of the small intestine, digestive juices pour forth. *Pancreatic juice* comes from a gland called the *pancreas*, and contains a number of enzymes. It contains a protein-splitting enzyme which continues the hydrolysis of proteins begun in the stomach. Pancreatic juice also contains an amylase which continues the breakdown of starch molecules begun in the mouth until maltose—containing only two glucose units—is formed. It also contains a lipase, which causes partial hydrolysis of fat molecules. The name *lipase* is a general one for enzymes which help in the splitting of fat molecules.

A second digestive juice called *bile* passes into the upper part of the small intestine. It comes from the liver, and though it contains no enzymes, it does contain salts. These convert fat (which is liquefied by the warmth of the stomach) into very small droplets, and this assists the action of fat-splitting enzymes, because a large surface area of fat is exposed to the enzyme surface.

The walls of the small intestine produce a digestive juice called *intestinal juice*. This contains enzymes which complete the hydrolysis of proteins into amino acids, and of starch into glucose.

The process of digestion is almost completed in the small intestine. Carbohydrates (except cellulose), proteins and fats are all in the form of small units, which are absorbed through the walls of the small intestine into the blood. Mineral elements, vitamins and water—which do not need to be broken down before they can be absorbed—are also absorbed at this stage.

Any food that has not been absorbed from the small intestine passes into a wider and shorter tube called the *large intestine*. No new enzymes are produced here, and no further digestion takes place. The main task of the large intestine is to remove water from undigested material. All the breakdown stages in digestion are hydrolyses and therefore involve the use of water. A great deal of water passes into the digestive system in the form of digestive juices, and it is important to recover this so that it can be used again. Water is absorbed in the large intestine and passes back into the tissues. After the removal of water, indigested material is removed from the body through the anus. One such material is cellulose and it is not digestible because, as we saw on page 24, it is difficult to hydrolyse, and so passes through the body unchanged. In spite of the fact that we cannot digest cellulose, its presence in our diet is important because it acts as *roughage*; i.e. it stimulates the muscular action of our intestines and so helps to prevent constipation.

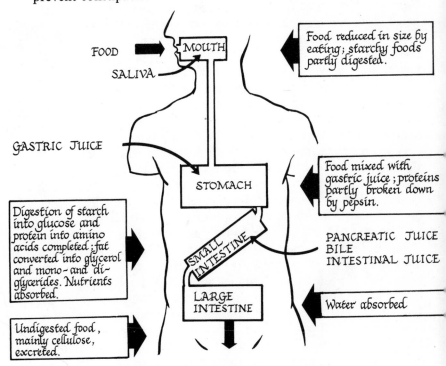

Fig. 16. Summary of the digestive process.

Disregard diagram. Put information on other diagram in your book.

SUMMARY

During digestion carbohydrates, proteins and fats are all broken down into much simpler molecules. This process is summarized in Fig. 16. In each case the breakdown process is a hydrolysis, and occurs in a large number of steps. Each step is assisted by a catalyst, which is nearly always an enzyme. Enzymes are proteins and act by providing a surface upon which molecules may come together and react.

Many different enzymes are used in digestion because an enzyme will only catalyse a very small number of reactions, and sometimes only one. After large nutrient molecules have been broken down into small ones by hydrolysis, they are absorbed into the bloodstream, a process which occurs mainly in the small intestine. Vitamins, mineral elements and water, which do not need to be digested are also absorbed in the small intestine. Material, such as cellulose, which is not absorbed passes through the body unchanged, and is excreted through the anus.

4 Energy Foods

Measuring Energy

Food supplies us with energy, and we are now going to see how we get energy from food and which foods give us the most energy. First, however, we must say a few words about measuring energy.

Energy may be measured as *heat*, and so we must be able to measure hotness.   The degree of hotness of something is called its *temperature*.   Temperature is measured with a thermometer, and is usually recorded in degrees *Centigrade*.   On the Centigrade scale we define the temperature at which water freezes as zero, and the temperature at which it boils as one hundred.   We write these temperatures 0°C. and 100°C.   We also use the *Fahrenheit* scale, though this is going out of favour.   On this scale the freezing point of water is 32 degrees (32°F.) and the boiling point of water is 212 degrees (212°F.).   Both temperature scales are shown below.

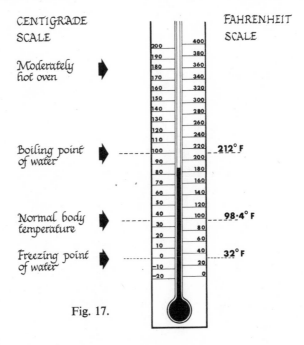

Fig. 17.

Just as we need a definite unit of temperature—the degree—so we also need a definite unit of energy. The most convenient unit of energy for measuring our bodies' energy needs, and the energy supplied by food is a unit of heat energy called the *large calorie* or *kilogram calorie*. This unit is defined as the amount of heat required to raise the temperature of 1,000 grams (just over 2 pounds) of water by 1°C. For simplicity we shall refer to this unit as a *Calorie*, or use the shortened form of *Cal*.

Energy Needed to Sustain Life

We saw in the first chapter that our bodies may be thought of as living machines, and that even at rest they are constantly using up energy to keep internal processes going. For instance, energy is used up in keeping our bodies warm and our hearts beating. It is also needed to sustain the continual activity of the millions of tiny cells that go to make up our bodies.

The energy needed to keep all our internal processes going is called the energy of *basal metabolism*, and you will find it discussed further on page 100. The energy of basal metabolism varies from person to person. Big people use up more energy than small people, men use up more than women and young people use up more than old. As an example, a young man of average build has a basal metabolism of about 1,700 Calories per day.

Energy Needed for Physical Activities

When we get up in the morning the rate at which we use up energy suddenly increases. Dressing, washing, going downstairs, eating breakfast—all use up energy. In fact *every* physical activity uses up energy. Even if we are lazy for a day we use up a large number of Calories; and if we are energetic—and perhaps play netball or go for a swim—we use up an even larger number.

In a similar way, people with energetic jobs, such as miners and farmers, use up larger numbers of Calories than people who sit at their work, such as typists and bus drivers. The chart shown in Fig. 18, shows that the more active a job is, the greater is the amount of energy used. The figures given are only average values, as they vary from person to person. For instance, a fat man uses up more energy in doing a particular job than does a thin person, and a woman uses up rather less than a man.

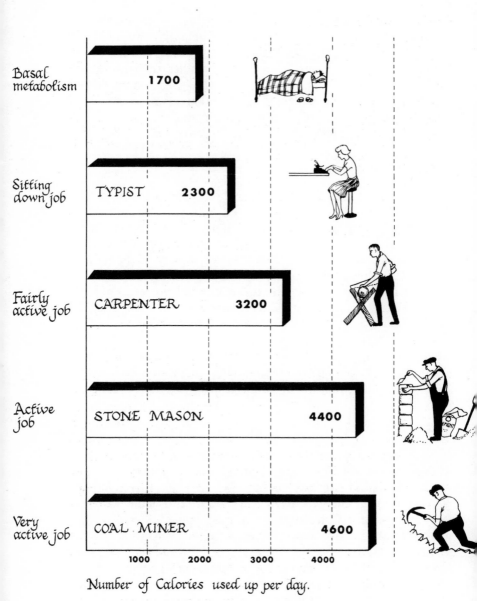

Number of Calories used up per day.

Fig. 18. The way energy needs vary with type of job.

Energy Value of Foods

Our energy needs must be supplied by food, and the amount of energy supplied by a food is called its *energy value*. We can express the energy or Calorie value of a food as the number of Calories that a given weight of the food will make available to our bodies.

The three types of nutrient which provide us with energy are carbohydrates, fats and proteins. We can give to each of these an average Calorie value, and these are shown below;

Nutrient	Average Calorie value	
	Cal./g.	Cal./oz.
Carbohydrate	4	116
Fat	9	263
Protein	4	116

If we eat a certain amount of fat it will give us more than twice as many Calories as the same weight of carbohydrate or protein. This means that fatty foods—such as butter and cheese—are more concentrated sources of Calories than mainly carbohydrate or protein foods such as potatoes and meat. Incidentally the difference in Calorie value between a hot meal and a cold meal is very small indeed compared with the Calorie value of the food itself.

Figure 19 shows the Calorie values of a number of foods. You will notice that fatty foods head the list, while foods containing a high proportion of water (which has no Calorie value), such as milk and tomatoes, come at the bottom. You will find another way of comparing the energy values of foods illustrated in Fig. 42 on page 113. In this diagram you can see the amounts of different foods you would have to eat to gain 100 Calories.

If you turn back to Fig. 2 on page 14, you will see that carbohydrates and fats have only one function, to provide us with energy. Proteins, on the other hand, are concerned with all the three functions of food. In fact the *main* purpose of protein foods is to act as body-builders, and so we shall discuss them separately in the next chapter.

45

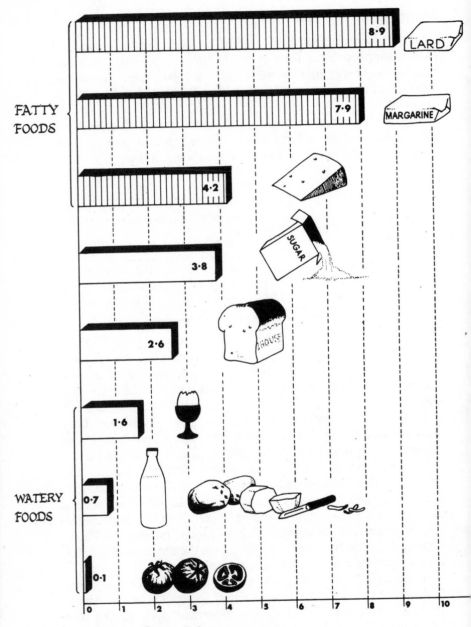

FATTY FOODS

WATERY FOODS

8·9 LARD
7·9 MARGARINE
4·2
3·8 SUGAR
2·6 HOUSE
1·6
0·7
0·1

0 1 2 3 4 5 6 7 8 9 10

Calorie value in Calories per gram.

Fig. 19.   The Calorie value of some foods.

46

The Way Food Supplies us with Energy

We obtain energy from food by oxidizing it. Oxidation can be thought of in a very simple way as the reaction of a substance with *oxygen*. In a car engine we have a similar type of reaction; petrol reacts with oxygen to produce a large amount of energy. This reaction happens so rapidly that it is really a small explosion. In our bodies the oxidation takes place much more slowly, but it is exactly the same *sort* of reaction.

Oxygen is brought into our bodies through the lungs and is carried round in the blood. Also in the blood is a small amount of dissolved *glucose*. Glucose is the basic source of human energy, and is produced during digestion of carbohydrate foods (except cellulose). Glucose and oxygen react together producing carbon dioxide, water and energy. (Fig. 20.)

As we need energy all the time, this reaction between glucose and oxygen never stops. This means that our bodies are constantly producing carbon dioxide and water (as vapour), and these gaseous waste products are removed from our bodies through the lungs.

You can sometimes see the water present in breath. When you breathe out on a cold frosty morning you can see the little cloud of water droplets that is formed when the water vapour from your breath is turned into water by the drop in temperature.

There is also a simple test for carbon dioxide; when it is bubbled through a clear solution of *lime water*, the solution turns milky.

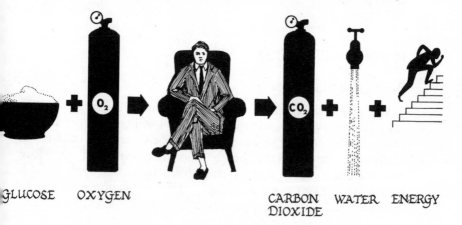

GLUCOSE   OXYGEN   CARBON   WATER   ENERGY
                                    DIOXIDE

Fig. 20. The reaction of glucose with oxygen inside our bodies.

If you blow through a tube which dips into a solution of lime water, you can easily see that the solution soon turns milky, proving that your breath contains carbon dioxide.

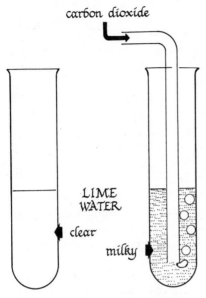

Fig. 21. The action of carbon dioxide on lime water.

You may be wondering how this reaction between glucose and oxygen is slowed down in our bodies so that we obtain a controlled supply of energy. The answer is that the process is controlled by enzymes called *oxidizing enzymes*. You will remember that in digestion, the process of hydrolysis takes place in a number of steps, and that each step is controlled by a hydrolysing enzyme. In the same way the reaction between glucose and oxygen takes place in a number of steps, each step being controlled by an oxidizing enzyme. As each step results in the release of a small amount of energy, the body receives the even flow of energy which it needs.

IMPORTANT ENERGY FOODS

Butter and Margarine

We have already noted that fatty foods are the most concentrated sources of energy in our diet. You will notice from Fig. 19 (page 46) that margarine has a high Calorie value; that of butter is about the same. Both butter and margarine are therefore valuable energy foods and, as we shall see, they also supply us with useful amounts of other nutrients. They are both important in our diet, and an average person eats about 6 oz. of butter and 4 oz. of margarine per week.

Butter is an animal fat made from cow's milk. Milk contains

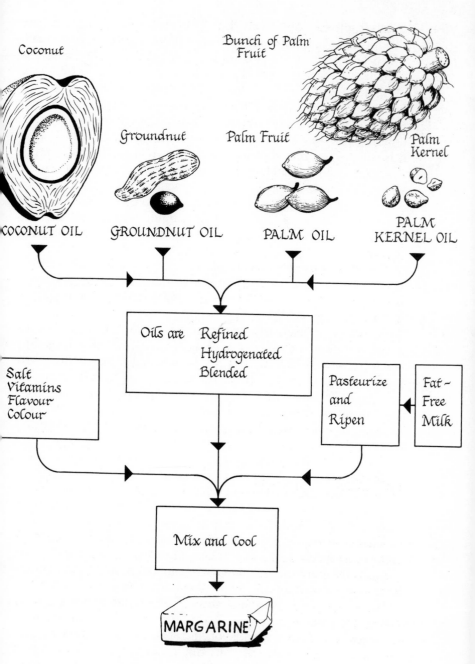

Fig. 22. The manufacture of margarine.

49

3

small droplets of oil, which rise to the surface when milk is kept and form the familiar 'cream layer'. Butter is made from cream which has been allowed to sour or 'ripen'. The sour cream is stirred or 'churned' until the oil drops have formed solid lumps of butter. The solid is removed from the liquid part—called butter milk—and salt and often colouring are added. The butter is then worked until a suitable consistency is obtained.

Butter has been a part of the British diet for centuries. Indeed it is hard to imagine our diet without it. During the last century the demand for animal fats—of which butter and lard are the most common—increased so fast that production could not keep pace with demand. There was no shortage of liquid vegetable oils, however, and a way of converting liquid oils into solid fats was sought and discovered at the beginning of the present century.

The conversion of liquid oils into solid fats is called *oil hardening*, and it is done by a process called *hydrogenation*. The difference between oils and fats is due to the difference in the amounts of unsaturated fatty acid units that they contain (page 30). Oils contain more of such acid units than fats. To convert an oil into a fat, therefore, we must change the *unsaturated* fatty acids into *saturated* ones. This can be done by reacting the oil with hydrogen. The reaction is slow at room temperature, but it can be speeded up by pumping in the hydrogen under pressure and warming the oil in the presence of a small amount of the metallic element, *nickel*. Nickel is a catalyst and so helps to speed up the reaction.

Margarine is an important fat made by hydrogenation of vegetable oils. Oils, such as *coconut oil*, *groundnut oil* and *palm oil*, are blended together, refined and hydrogenated. The hydrogenated oils are mixed with ripened milk, from which the cream has been removed. An emulsifying agent—which aids the formation of an emulsion—is added and mixing is continued until an emulsion (see p. 73) which looks like thick white cream is obtained. On cooling, the emulsion becomes solid, and this is worked until it has a smooth even texture.

In order to improve the flavour of margarine and make it as similar as possible to butter, various substances are added to it during its manufacture. Flavouring agents and salt are added to try and produce a butter flavour and a yellow dye is added to give it a butter colour. Also, vitamins A and D are added in such

Butter Manufacture. (1) Cream passes through pasteurizers (background) into large tanks (foreground) where it is allowed to ripen. (2) Cream is churned in rotating vessels and forms a granular solid. (3) When the butter is of the proper consistency it is removed from the churn. (4) The butter is packed in automatic machines.

quantities that margarine contains at least as much of these vitamins as butter.

The nutritional value of margarine is about the same as that of butter. They are both about four-fifths fat and one-fifth water and in addition they both contain valuable amounts of vitamins A and D. Margarine is as good a food as butter and it may be better, because it has a fixed vitamin content, whereas that of butter varies, being higher in summer than in winter.

Wheat and Milling

Of all the cultivated grasses known as *cereals*, wheat is the most important in Britain. Wheat is now grown in most parts of the world, from tropical regions such as India to temperate regions such as the prairies of Canada, and even to the cold areas bordering on the Arctic Circle. It is, of course, grown in Britain and fields of gently-waving golden wheat are among the loveliest sights of the late summer.

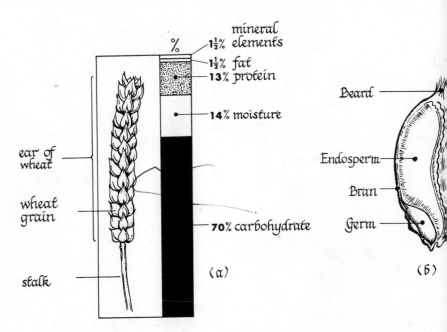

Fig. 23.   (a) The composition of wheat and (b) the structure of a wheat grain (as a section through the germ).

52

When wheat is threshed the wheat *grains* are separated from the stalks and the chaff.   An average grain of wheat is about a quarter of an inch long and an eighth of an inch broad.   As you can see from Fig. 23 a wheat grain is roughly egg-shaped, with a number of small hairs, called the *beard*, at one end.   There are three main parts of a wheat grain; the seed or *germ*, the *endosperm* which makes up about 90% of the grain, and a tough outer skin called the bran.

The bran is mainly composed of cellulose.   It is therefore indigestible and is normally removed before wheat is used as a food. The germ is rich in nutrients, particularly protein, fat, the B group of vitamins and iron.   The endosperm is mainly starch, the spaces between the starch grains being filled with protein.   The actual composition of different types of wheat varies a good deal, but average values are given in Fig. 23.   You will see from these figures that the main nutrient in wheat is carbohydrate, and for this reason wheat is usually regarded as an energy food.   Indeed, food products made from wheat provide most people with about one-fifth of their Calories.

Whole grains of wheat are difficult to digest because of their outer cellulose layer.   It is therefore usual to remove the bran and convert the grains into a powdery flour before they are used as food.   This process is known as *milling*, and in essence it consists of removing the bran and germ, and grinding the endosperm into powder with rollers.   The actual process is very complex, however, and we shall only be able to give a brief outline of it here.

Before milling starts different varieties of wheat are blended together in such a way that the resulting flour has the properties needed for the purpose for which it is to be used.   It is then cleaned, so that small stones, dust, chaff and so on are removed. In the first stage of milling the wheat grains are passed through a series of rollers with corrugated surfaces.   The rollers are arranged in pairs and the rollers of each pair rotate in opposite directions and at different speeds.   As the grains pass between the rollers, they are torn open and the endosperm released.   Each pair of rollers is set closer together than the preceding pair, so that the endosperm is ground into increasingly small particles.   The branny material is removed by sieving, and the endosperm is passed through a series of smooth rollers which convert it into a fine powder.   Finally the powder is sieved and this removes the germ, which is flattened, rather than powdered, by the smooth rollers.

Types of Flour

The milling process can be modified to give more or less flour from a given amount of wheat. The percentage of flour obtained is called the *extraction rate* of the flour. For example, true *wholemeal* flour has an extraction rate of 100%, meaning that the whole grain has been converted into flour. It gets its brown colour from a pigment in the bran. As the extraction rate is lowered, the proportion of bran remaining in the flour decreases and so the colour becomes lighter and the flour more digestible. A typical white flour in use to-day has an extraction rate of 70% and such a flour contains almost nothing but crushed endosperm.

As the extraction rate goes down, so does the amount of vitamins and mineral elements in the flour. The proportion of bran and germ in the resulting flour is also reduced. Thus such flour contains less mineral elements (particularly iron) and vitamins (particularly vitamins of the B group) than flour of a higher extraction rate. It also contains somewhat reduced amounts of protein and calcium.

In view of these facts you may wonder why we normally eat bread made from white flour rather than from wholemeal or brown flour. The real reason why we do this is that we prefer a white loaf to a dark-coloured loaf. Since very early times white bread has been a symbol of prosperity. As far back as Roman times white bread was eaten by rich people of the towns, whereas the poorer countryfolk had to be content with the cheaper wholemeal loaf. Thus white bread was prized because it was an expensive luxury; also because most people associated whiteness with purity. Nowadays we do not regard white bread as a luxury—indeed we take it for granted—but we still tend to feel that a fine white flour is 'purer' than a coarse brown one.

At this point you may be sadly resolving to eat more brown bread in future. But before you come to any such decision there is another factor to be considered. It is certainly true that wholemeal flour has a greater vitamin and mineral element content than white flour, but it is also true that wholemeal flour is less digestible than white flour, because of the indigestible bran that it contains. Also the nutrients in wholemeal flour may not be so well absorbed into the body as those in white flour. This is because there is more of a substance called *phytic acid* in brown flour than in white. Phytic acid combines with calcium and iron in the flour

to form insoluble salts which the body cannot absorb. Luckily some of the phytic acid in flour is broken down during baking, and so the loss of nutrients due to this cause is not very great.

What we have just said will suggest to you that the superiority of the wholemeal flour over white is not so obvious as it seemed at first sight. However, the fact remains that during the milling of white flour, nutrients are lost. For this reason certain nutrients are now added to all flour in this country—except 100% whole-meal—to make good the losses that occur during milling. The vitamins *thiamine* and *nicotinic acid*, and the mineral elements *iron* and *calcium* (in the form of chalk) are added in sufficient quantities to ensure that the amounts present will be equivalent to the amounts in flour of 80% extraction rate. In the case of calcium the amount present will greatly exceed that in such 80% flour. In fact there is enough calcium to react with all the phytic acid present *and* leave some over for us!

You will probably agree now, that you may safely go on eating white bread; indeed it is a most valuable food. Not only is it valuable as an energy food, but it also provides an average person with about a fifth of the protein, calcium and iron in his diet and nearly a quarter of the thiamine and nicotinic acid.

Bread

If you think for a moment of a freshly-baked loaf of bread with its delicious smell, its light open texture and its crisp brown crust, you will realize that great changes occur when bread is made from flour.

Bread is made from flour, water, yeast and salt. There are many ways in which these ingredients can be converted into bread; all we can do here is to give an outline of the main principles involved. Then we shall describe the practical details of *one* way of making bread.

When flour and water are mixed together, dough is formed and proteins in the flour form an elastic substance called *gluten*, which binds together the flour in the dough. In biblical times this dough was simply baked to give a hard and unattractive product called *unleavened bread*. In order to make bread as we know it to-day, the dough must be made lighter by puffing it up with gas. This process is called *aeration*.

Bloomer

Rolls

Split Tin

Cottage

Wholemeal Cob

Coburg

Cholla or Plait

Vienna

Rolls

Fruit

Types of bread

STAGES IN MAKING HOME-MADE WHITE BREAD

Stages	Description
Choice and proportions of ingredients	3½ lb. flour (plain, white and strong; see page 141), 1 oz. fresh yeast, 1½ pints water, 4 teaspoons salt.
Possible additional ingredients	In milk bread water is partly or wholly replaced by milk, and a little fat is added to the mixture. This gives a loaf of more flavour, smoother texture, softer crumb and better keeping qualities.
Preparation of ingredients	The yeast is mixed with warm water (about 85°F.). The flour is sifted into a warmed basin and the salt mixed in; the basin is kept in a warm place.
Mixing	A hollow is made in the flour and the liquid poured in. The mixture is well stirred to form a soft dough.
Kneading	The dough is put onto a floured board and worked well with the knuckles. This stretches the gluten and disperses the yeast evenly through the mixture, so assisting the next stage.
Proving	The dough is put back into the basin, which is covered and put into a warm place. It is left there until fermentation has doubled the size of the dough (1–1½ hours).
Knocking back	The risen dough is kneaded or 'knocked back' on a floured board. This gives the dough an extra mixing, and the right degree of firmness.
Moulding	The dough is moulded into the weight, and later the shape, required. If a tin is used, this is greased, warmed and half filled with dough.
Reproving	Moulding expels some gas, so the mixture is now allowed to stand in a warm place until the dough has again doubled its size.
Baking	The dough is put into a hot oven for 30–50 minutes, the actual time depending upon the size of the loaf.
Testing the baked loaf	After removal from the oven the loaf is tapped on its underside. If it is properly baked it gives a hollow sound.

Making bread on a large scale. (1) Flour, fat, water, mixed together. (2) The dough is taken from the mixer and (3) rolled into balls and allowed to ferment. (4) It is cut again, (5) twisted, put into greased tins and proved again. (6) It moves through the oven and is cooked.

The gas used for aeration is carbon dioxide, and it is produced by *fermentation*. Fermentation processes are brought about by enzymes and in this case the enzymes are contained within very small living cells of yeast. Yeast cells are too small to be seen with the naked eye, but they are clearly visible through a microscope. They live and multiply by using the protein of the dough as food. They also use the sugars present in the dough to obtain energy. In using the sugar they break it down into carbon dioxide and *alcohol*, the substance which is present in all alcoholic drinks, such as beer and wines. The carbon dioxide produced in this way becomes trapped in the dough as small pockets of gas.

Yeast is added during dough-making and when the dough has been divided up into lumps of the desired weight, it is put into the oven to be baked. In the oven the dough first rises rapidly because the pockets of trapped gas expand as the gas gets hot. Fermentation continues until the temperature of the aerated dough reaches about 130°F. At this temperature the yeast cells are killed.

The gradual expansion of the dough is made possible because of the eleastic nature of the gluten. As gluten is made from proteins, it coagulates when it gets hot. Thus during baking the elasticity of the loaf is lost and its shape becomes fixed. The nature of the starch also changes as it gets hot. It absorbs water to such an extent that the starch grains swell and burst—a process which is discussed more fully on page 133. Owing to the high temperature on the outside of the loaf, the starch is converted into a hard crust which, if baked sufficiently, is crisp and golden-brown in colour.

Bread is cooked for 30–50 minutes, depending upon its size, and the result is the familiar loaf of bread—so familiar in fact that we are apt to forget that it has needed much skill and effort to produce it from those fields of golden wheat.

Other Cereals

Although wheat is the most important cereal eaten in Great Britain, a number of others are used and their energy value and uses are summarized in the table on the next page.

Comparing the Calorie values given in the table, it will be seen that oats has the highest energy value. Between them, cereals

COMPARISON OF CEREALS

	Form in which cereal is used for food	Calorie value per ounce	Cooked forms	Manufactured food products
Wheat	Wheat flour (white)	100	Bread, buns, cakes, biscuits	Bread, semolina, puffed wheat, grapenuts
Oats	Oatmeal	115	Parkin, porridge, oat-cakes	Breakfast cereals, e.g. oat crunchies
Rye	Rye flour	95	Rye bread	Rye bread, Ryvita
Barley	Pearl barley	102	Added to some soups and stews	Malt, barley water
Maize	Maize flour	101	Corn-on-the-cob	Corn flakes, cornflour, custard and blancmange powders
Rice	Rice flour (groundrice), Polished rice	102	Rice puddings, savoury rice dishes	Breakfast cereals, e.g. rice crispies

provide more than one-third of the energy value of our diet. In addition they supply us with valuable amounts of protein, calcium, iron and the B vitamins. The difference in the appearance of these cereals is shown in Fig. 24.

Potatoes

Potatoes are so much a part of our everyday diet, that it comes as rather a surprise to learn that they were only introduced into England towards the end of the sixteenth century. Even more surprising is the fact that the people of England were so suspicious of them that they did not become a normal part of our English

60

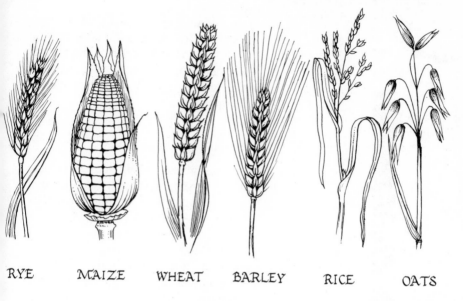

RYE　　MAIZE　　WHEAT　　BARLEY　　RICE　　OATS

Fig. 24.

diet until another two hundred years had passed. Nowadays it is unusual for a day to go by when we do *not* eat potatoes during at least one of our meals.

When potatoes are growing the only part that is visible is the green leafy part. It is here that the plant manufactures its food supply, which consists mainly of starch. The potato is classified as a *tuber* because this food material is stored in a swollen stem or tuber which develops underground. When we eat potatoes, we are really eating the reserve food supply of the plant.

Potatoes contain about 15% to 20% starch, the remainder being mainly water together with small amounts of proteins, mineral elements and vitamins. Potatoes are mainly prized as an energy food, though their Calorie value is only 75 Cal./100 g. If you refer back to Fig. 19 on page 46 you will see that this is a low value, and that bread, for example, provides about three times as much energy as an equal weight of potatoes. Nevertheless, if we eat large quantities of potatoes they are a useful source of Calories—and also of proteins.

Potatoes contain only small amounts of vitamins, the main one being vitamin C (ascorbic acid). When potatoes are peeled and cooked, some of the vitamin C is lost, yet in spite of this potatoes

61

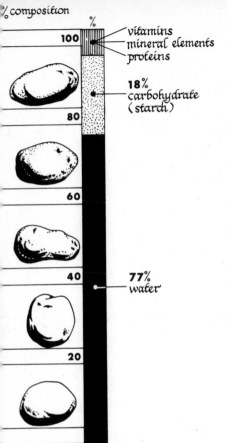

% composition

100 — vitamins, mineral elements, proteins

18% carbohydrate (starch)

80

60

77% water

40

20

Fig. 25. The average nutrient content of potatoes.

supply an average person with about *one-third* of his total intake of this vitamin. Potatoes also contain small amounts of the vitamins thiamine and nicotinic acid, and the mineral element iron.

Other Vegetables

Vegetables, other than potatoes, are poor energy foods, but they are useful sources of vitamins, particularly of vitamins A and C. For example, root vegetables such as carrots are valuable sources of vitamin A, green vegetables such as cabbage and sprouts provide us with vitamins A and C, and pulses such as peas and beans contain vitamin A and some B vitamins. Bulbs, such as onions and leeks, have very little nutritional value and are mainly prized for their flavour.

Sugar

Sugar may be extracted either from sugar-*beet* or from sugar-*cane*, but whichever source is used, the product obtained is the same. Sugar-cane, which grows only in tropical countries, is a type of giant grass. It resembles bamboo and may grow as high as 20 feet. Sugar-beet, which grows in temperate climates such as Britain, has a large white-pink root in which the sugar is stored.

Sucrose is extracted from sugar cane by crushing the cane and spraying it with water. The solution obtained contains the sucrose and also some impurities. The impurities are removed by boiling the solution, adding lime and filtering. The clear solution which is left is concentrated until a mixture of sugar crystals and liquid—called *molasses*—is formed. The liquid is removed by spinning the mixture in a machine rather like a spin drier. It consists of a

Contrasts in harvesting sugar cane. *Top:* Cutting by hand (Jamaica).
Bottom: Mechanical harvesting (Australia).

drum containing holes, through which the liquid escapes. If sugar beet is the starting material, the procedure is similar, except that the sucrose is extracted from the beet by shredding it, and by steeping the shredded beet in hot water.

Raw sugar, whether obtained from cane or beet, still contains some impurities and these are removed in the next part of the process. The raw sugar is redissolved in water, and carbon dioxide is bubbled through the solution and lime added to remove impurities. The resulting brownish solution is decolourized by passing it through a bed of charcoal, and concentrated by heating in 'vacuum pans'. During the concentration process sugar crystals form, and the liquid is removed by spinning as before. The liquid, which is rich in sugar, is used for making golden syrup or brown sugar.

Sugar in crystalline form as obtained by the above method is almost pure sucrose, the nature and properties of which were discussed in Chapter 2. In addition to normal granulated sugar, other types are produced and graded according to crystal size. *Lump sugar* is a form of granulated sugar in which the crystals are bound together in a solid mass. The mass is cut into cubes of any desired size by machines, any fragments being sold as *preserving sugar*. *Caster sugar* contains smaller crystals than granulated sugar, and *icing sugar* contains even smaller crystals, obtained by grinding granulated sugar to a powder.

Confectionery

Boiled sweets, toffee and chocolate are all sugar products and therefore useful energy foods. Many of us have a 'sweet tooth' and have a tendency to eat more sweets than is good for us. If we eat too many sweets, we may suffer several bad effects. For example, if we do not use up the energy gained from the sweets, we get fat. Also too many sweets dull our appetite, and so we may not feel like eating our normal meals. Lastly, sweets are bad for our teeth and make frequent visits to the dentist necessary.

Chocolate is a very nutritious type of confectionery being made from cocoa, cocoa-butter and sugar (and dried or condensed milk in milk chocolate). Chocoate is rich in both sugar and fat and in addition it contains useful amounts of iron, calcium, vitamin A and the B vitamins.

SUMMARY

Food supplies us with energy which we need both for maintaining our internal processes—the energy of basal metabolism—and for physical activities. The energy given us by a food is called its energy or Calorie value and it is measured in large or kilogram calories. Fats, carbohydrates and proteins all supply us with energy, though proteins are mainly *body-builders. Fats have more than twice the Calorie value of the other two. We obtain energy from food after it has been digested by oxidizing it with the help of oxidizing enzymes.*

Butter and margarine both have about the same nutritional value, being about four-fifths fat. They are therefore both concentrated sources of Calories. Butter is made by churning ripened cream; margarine, by hardening vegetable oils by hydro-genation.

Oats, barley and maize are examples of cultivated grasses called cereals. The most important cereal in our diet, however, is wheat. Wheat grains are converted into flour by milling, when the outer parts of the grain—the bran and germ—are removed and the remaining endosperm is ground into a powder. Most flour we use to-day has an extraction rate of 70%, meaning that 30% of the grain has been lost during milling. To replace nutrients lost in milling, vitamins (thiamine and nicotinic acid) and mineral elements (iron and calcium) are added to the flour.

Bread is made from flour, water, yeast and salt. A dough of flour and water is aerated during baking by carbon dioxide produced by the fermentation of yeast. During baking the dough rises and its shape becomes fixed when the proteins present coagulate.

Potatoes are the most valuable vegetable in our diet. They are four-fifths water but, because we eat considerable amounts, they do supply us with a large proportion of our vitamin C intake as well as useful amounts of carbohydrate and protein. The main virtue of most other vegetables that we eat is that they supply us with useful amounts of vitamins; otherwise they are mainly water.

Sugar is extracted from either sugar cane or sugar beet and the product is almost pure sucrose. In addition to granulated sugar several other forms are made such as caster and icing sugar. Sugar forms a large part of confectionery products, such as boiled sweets, toffee and chocolate, and these are therefore useful energy foods.

5 Body-building Foods

Your body is continually growing and therefore needs a plentiful supply of body-building material. When you are fully grown you will need a smaller supply of body-building nutrients, but you will still need enough to replace worn and damaged tissues and to build small amounts of new material, such as nails and hair. Our bodies are made up of millions of tiny cells; each of which is only about 1/10th millimetre in diameter. One of the most exciting recent developments in science is the development of an instrument—the *electron microscope*—that enables us to see what such cells are like.

The photograph below shows a single cell magnified about 20,000 times. Every cell contains *protein*, which is therefore one of the most important body-building nutrients. Groups of cells are built up into tissues, some of which are hard and some of which are soft. Bones and teeth are the most important hard tissues and are made of calcium phosphate built from oxygen and the mineral elements *calcium* and *phosphorus*. Muscle and nerve tissues are examples of soft tissues and these also contain mineral elements of which *iron*, *phosphorus* and *sulphur* are the most important.

It is clear that the main body-building nutrients are protein and some mineral elements (Fig. 26), though, as we shall see in the next chapter, they cannot always be used by the body without the assistance of vitamins, water and other mineral elements.

A typical cell (× 20,000).

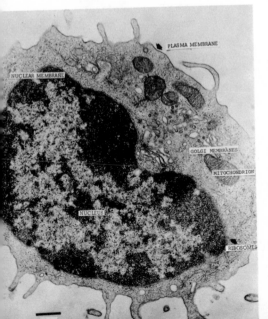

NUCLEAR MEMBRANE

PLASMA MEMBRANE

GOLGI MEMBRANES

MITOCHONDRION

NUCLEUS

RIBOSOMES

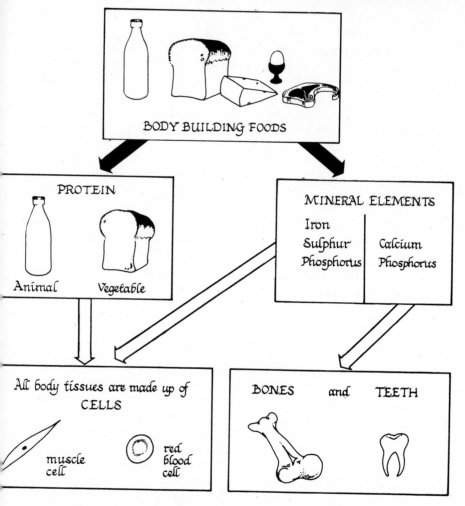

Fig. 26.   Body-building foods are needed for the growth and maintenance of bone and tissues.

Animal and Vegetable Protein

Protein molecules, as we saw in Chapter 2, are very large molecules made from many *amino acid* units.   About twenty different amino acids are found in protein molecules, though no single protein contains them all.   If an adult is provided with *eight* of these amino acids in his food, his body can make the other amino acids that it needs for itself.   A growing person needs *ten* of these amino acids, which are called *essential* amino acids.

Our diet *must* supply us with enough essential amino acids, because our bodies either cannot make them at all or cannot make them fast enough for our needs. It is clear that we must judge protein foods according as to whether they do or do not supply us with all the essential amino acids. Foods which do supply all the essential amino acids have high nutritive value, while those in which one or more essential amino acids are missing have low nutritive value.

We find that most protein food of animal origin is of high nutritive value. Meat, fish, milk and cheese are all good examples. On the other hand most protein of vegetable origin lacks at least one essential amino acid, and therefore has low nutritive value. There are exceptions to this general rule, and the proteins of *soya beans* for example contain all the essential amino acids. On the other hand *gelatin*, which is an animal protein obtained by boiling bones or gristle, is of low nutritive value.

Protein Foods and the Diet

A diet in which the only protein present was gelatin would be useless, because it would be lacking in some of the essential amino acids. To ensure that we receive enough of all the essential amino acids, a good proportion—about one-half—of the protein in our diet should be animal protein. If we ate nothing but vegetable protein (see vegetarian diet, page 124) we might well go short of some essential amino acids. This does not mean, of course, that vegetable protein is useless, but it does mean that vegetable protein should be eaten along with animal protein. In this way we receive a variety of different amino acids in the right sort of proportions for our body's needs.

Our bodies cannot store protein, and if they receive more than they need for body-building they use the remainder as a source of energy. It is therefore bad planning to have plenty of protein one day and none the next, because most of it will be used for energy, and we shall go short of protein for body-building. Diets should be planned so that *every* meal contains a proportion of protein and if possible about half of this should be animal protein. If the amount of animal protein available is limited, it should be spread out over as many meals as possible, and eaten with plenty of vegetable protein. Bread and cheese; milk and cereals; eggs, ham

or fish eaten with chips are all useful combinations, which provide a mixture of animal and vegetable protein.

It is important to get some idea of which foods are good sources of protein. In Fig. 27 you will see some of the most important protein foods in our diet. Each portion of food shown represents the amount needed to provide one-fifth the daily allowance of protein for a girl, thirteen to fifteen years old. You should notice which foods have a high protein content (e.g. soya flour and cheese) and which have a low one (e.g. potatoes).

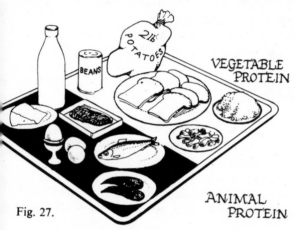

Vegetable protein

Soya flour, $1\frac{3}{4}$ oz.
Peanuts, $2\frac{1}{4}$ oz.
White bread, 8 oz.
Baked beans, 11 oz.
Potatoes, 32 oz.

Animal protein

Milk, 1 pint
Cheese, $2\frac{1}{2}$ oz.
Liver, $3\frac{1}{2}$ oz.
Cod, 4 oz.
Beef, $4\frac{1}{2}$ oz.
Eggs, $5\frac{1}{4}$ oz.

Fig. 27.

The foods shown in Fig. 27 have been divided up into animal and vegetable protein, and this will remind you that in meal planning, protein of both types should be included. It will also remind you that although six slices of bread and one pint of milk contain the same *amount* of protein, the *value* of the milk protein for body-building is much greater than that of the bread.

Mineral Elements for Body-building

Calcium and phosphorus are the two main mineral elements that we need for body-building. Phosphorus is present in a wide variety of foods, and any normal diet will supply our needs. Cheese, milk, meat, fish and oatmeal are all good sources of phosphorus. Calcium, on the other hand, is not present in large amounts in many foodstuffs, and proper diet planning is needed to ensure that we obtain enough. Milk and milk products are the

best sources of calcium in our diet, and they supply well over half our total intake. Calcium is added to all flour (except wholemeal) in this country to make sure we do not go short of calcium. Thus bread, biscuits, cakes and all foods made from flour are good sources of calcium.

Food	Amount
Milk	1 pint
Dried skimmed milk	2 oz.
Cheese	3 oz.
Sardines	6 oz.
White flour	16 oz.
Kippers	20 oz.
Eggs	20 oz.
White bread	22 oz.

Fig. 28.

If you look at Fig. 28 you will see the amount of different foods needed to supply half the calcium allowance of a girl aged thirteen to fifteen. When you plan meals, you should include some of the foods shown each day so that our calcium needs are met.

Figure 29 shows three combinations of food that would supply enough calcium for one day for a girl between thirteen and fifteen.

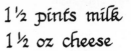

1½ pints milk
1½ oz cheese

1 pint milk
3 oz sardines
1½ oz cheese

1½ pints milk
2 eggs
4 slices of bread

Fig. 29.

You will notice that each suggestion includes milk as the main source of calcium. All diets should include at least one pint of milk daily, while for children, adolescents, and women during pregnancy and when nursing babies, extra milk is highly desirable.

IMPORTANT BODY-BUILDING FOODS

Milk and cheese; meat and fish; bread and other foods made from flour; eggs—these are the main body-building foods in our diet. In addition to being body-builders bread and flour are also important sources of energy, and as such were discussed in the last chapter.

Milk

Of all the foods in our diet, milk is the finest. When we talk of milk, we normally mean cow's milk and though we could not live on it alone—it is not a *perfect* food—it is nevertheless a rich source of nutrients (see page 72).

The nutrient content of milk is shown in Fig. 30, and you will notice that it contains every class of nutrient. In spite of this, milk is nearly nine-tenths water and you might be tempted to class it with drinks, such as fruit squash or tea. However, this would

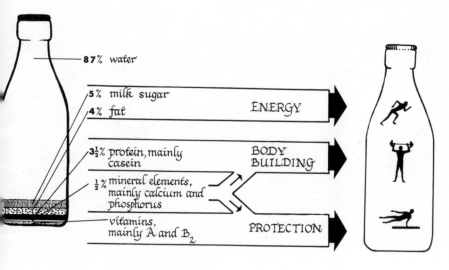

Fig. 30. The nutrient content of milk.

Although milk is not a perfect food it is one of the most valuable in our diet.

be a great mistake! Milk is much more than a pleasant drink, because the 13% of solid material that it contains supply us with valuable nutrients in their most digestible form.

Milk as a body-builder. Milk is prized mainly as a body-building food. If you turn back to Figs. 27 and 28 (pages 69 and 70) you will see that one pint of milk per day supplies a girl of 13 to 15 with one-fifth of her protein allowance and half of her calcium allowance. It also supplies useful amounts of phosphorus. But the body-building value of milk is even greater than these figures suggest. The quantity of protein in milk is not great but what it lacks in quantity it makes up for in quality. All the proteins in milk are of high nutritive value, the most important being *casein*. This is a conjugated protein (see page 28) containing phosphorus. In addition milk proteins are easily digested, so that little is lost through incomplete digestion.

During digestion milk becomes solid, because in the stomach an enzyme called *rennin* coagulates casein into a hard clot. You can make milk clot very easily yourself if you warm a little to blood-heat in a pan and add *rennet* (which is a preparation containing rennin). You will see the milk slowly turning into a white solid, from which oozes a slightly yellow liquid called *whey*. You have in fact made *junket*, which makes an easily-digested and nutritious pudding.

Energy nutrients in milk. You know that when milk is allowed to stand for a time a layer of cream forms at the top. The fat in milk is in the form of very tiny droplets. They are so small that a single drop of milk contains several million of them. When milk is shaken the oil drops become dispersed through the milk, but on standing the oil drops rise to the surface and form a layer. Such a mixture of droplets dispersed in another liquid is called an *emulsion* (other well-known emulsions are mayonnaise, salad dressings and creamed cake mixes). The fact that milk fat is in the form of an emulsion makes it very easy to digest.

The carbohydrate of milk is in the form of the sugar *lactose*, also called *milk sugar*. Milk sugar is only very slightly sweet, which is fortunate because we soon tire of sweet foods. As it is, the flavour of milk is very mild so that we do not tire of it, and it can be used in the preparation of many cooked dishes without giving them a 'milk flavour'.

73

Milk contains bacteria and easily 'sours' when it is stored. This is because enzymes in the bacteria convert milk sugar into a sour-tasting acid called *lactic acid*. This acid coagulates the casein in milk and turns it into a solid called *curds*. Now you will understand why it is important to have fresh milk supplies daily, and why milk must be stored carefully (see page 167).

Milk *curdles* more rapidly when it is warm than when it is cold, and so only fresh milk should be kept hot. For example, if you want to prepare a thermos flask of hot coffee for a picnic, use fresh milk. If you do not, you may find that when you open the flask you have an unpleasant curdled mass! The presence of acid hastens curdling, and so you need to take care when preparing such dishes as tomato soup, because the acidity of the tomato juice may be enough to curdle the hot milk.

The amount of fat and milk sugar in milk is small. Yet although milk does not have a high Calorie value, you can see from Fig. 31 that it makes a useful contribution to our Calorie intake. If a child aged two to five consumed two pints of milk a day, this would supply *half* her Calorie needs.

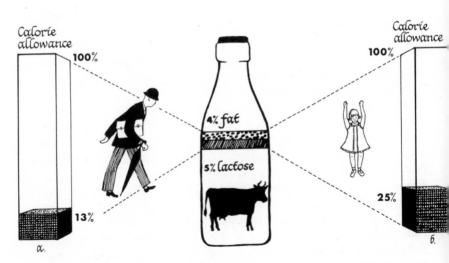

Fig. 31. One pint of milk daily contributes (a) 13% of the Calorie allowance of a fairly active man and (b) 25% of the Calorie allowance of a two- to five-year-old girl.

Protective nutrients in milk.　Milk is a valuable source of several vitamins.　The oil droplets contain vitamins A and D, while the watery part of the milk is rich in vitamin B_2 and also contains useful amounts of vitamins B_1 and C.　Unfortunately some of these vitamins may be destroyed before the milk reaches us if it is not carefully treated.　For example, if you leave your milk on the doorstep in the sun for several hours, you will destroy most of the vitamins B_2 and C.　Also if you heat milk for any length of time you will destroy some of the vitamins B_1 and C.

We have already noted that milk is a good source of calcium and phosphorus.　Unfortunately it is a poor source of iron. Cows' milk contains less iron than human milk and so, for example, when young babies are bottle-fed iron-rich foods should be added to the diet (see page 121).

Treatment of Milk.　Milk is such a rich source of nutrients that it is an ideal place for the growth of bacteria.　Although milk should be nearly free of bacteria at the time it is obtained from a clean healthy cow, it is impossible to keep it in this condition.　Bacteria from the person who milks the cow (or the milking machine), from the milk churn and from the air pass into the milk, where they settle down happily to grow and multiply!　Most of these bacteria are harmless and do nothing more than turn the milk sour. Bacteria from unhealthy cows, however, may well be harmful and cause tuberculosis.　In the past thousands of people and cattle have died each year in Great Britain alone from this cause.

Milk is such an important food that we must make sure that a supply of clean, fresh milk is available for everyone.　We are very lucky in Britain to-day that this is so and that milk arrives on our doorsteps as regularly as the newspaper.　We can make sure that milk is safe by means of heat treatment and by creating herds of cows in which harmful bacteria are absent.

The most common forms of heat treatment are pasteurization and sterilization, which are described on page 156.　Pasteurization of milk kills most bacteria present and is of great benefit in giving us safe milk.　It also destroys small amounts of vitamins B_1 and C, but this loss is of very little importance compared to the benefit of having clean wholesome milk always available.

The flavour of pasteurized milk is so similar to that of untreated milk that it is almost impossible to tell the difference between them.

The one disadvantage of pasteurized milk is that it does not keep long. Sterilized milk, however, keeps longer because it has been given a more severe heat treatment. If has a different flavour from fresh milk, and for this reason many people do not like it. New processes, however, can produce sterilized milk that will keep for months and that tastes similar to pasteurized milk. Sterilization produces a bigger loss of vitamins than pasteurization but this loss is not important. There is probably a big future for sterilized milk because it can cut down milk deliveries to once a week or even once a month.

You will remember that milk is nearly nine-tenths water, and it is therefore a very bulky food and so expensive to transport. Some of this water may be removed by evaporation to produce *evaporated milk* or, if sugar is added, *sweetened condensed milk*. The evaporation is carried out at a low temperature (below 150°F.) to avoid giving the milk a cooked flavour and to prevent coagulation of proteins. Such milk is sealed in cans and keeps until the can is opened.

Evaporated milk contains about 25% less water than fresh milk, but it is still a rather watery food. Most of the water in milk is removed in the production of *dried milk*, which is a powder. Dried milk is very rich in nutrients and by looking at Fig. 28, you can see, for example, that two ounces of dried milk contains as much calcium as a pint of fresh milk.

The conversion of fresh liquid milk into a powder enables milk to be kept for considerable periods in the most concentrated form possible. Liquid milk may also be converted into other solid foods that have good keeping qualities. The most important are butter, discussed in the last chapter, and cheese.

Cheese

How many types of cheese do you know? You will easily be able to think of about ten—or perhaps even twenty—but you will still be a long way from the total, which is the surprisingly large number of four hundred. In Great Britain alone many different varieties of cheese are made, and some of the best known of these are shown in Fig. 32.

British cheeses vary from very soft home-made cream cheeses to hard cheeses such as Cheddar; from white-coloured Stilton to

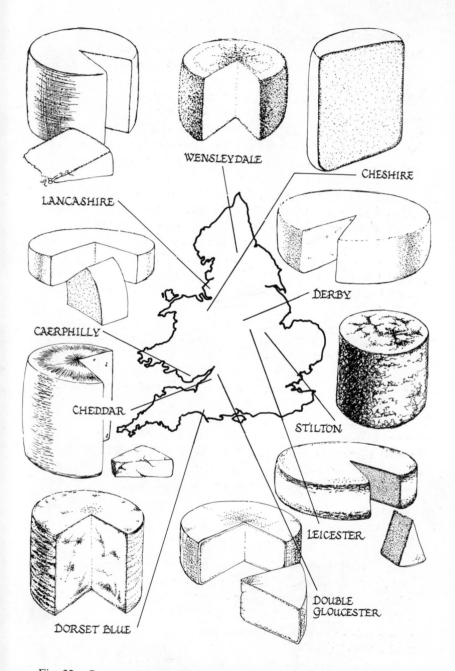

WENSLEYDALE

CHESHIRE

LANCASHIRE

DERBY

CAERPHILLY

CHEDDAR

STILTON

LEICESTER

DORSET BLUE

DOUBLE
GLOUCESTER

Fig. 32. Some well-known British cheeses and where they come from.

77

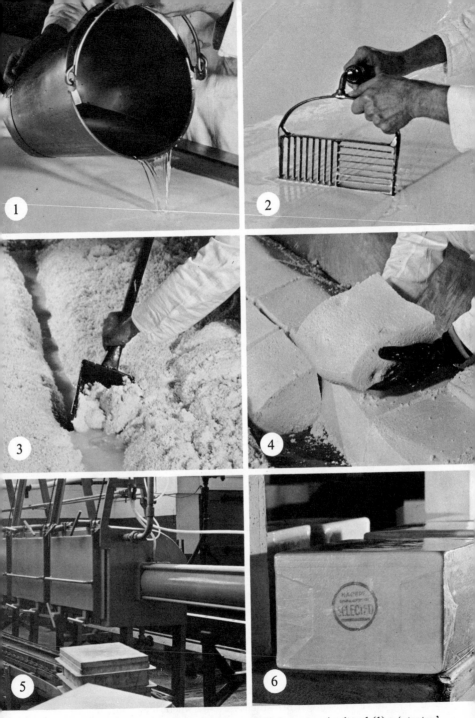

Fig. 33.   Making cheddar cheese.   Milk is pasteurized and (1) a 'starter' added to turn it sour; it is warmed and rennet added.   (2) The milk clots into solid curd which is cut into pieces and (3) the liquid remaining is drained off.   (4) The curd is turned and cut into small pieces; (5) pressed in moulds and (6) stored until mature.

pink Cheshire; from mild-flavoured Caerphilly to strong blue Stilton. Cheese can be eaten with many different foods—raw or cooked—to form tasty and nutritious dishes. Cheese cooked with cauliflower, cheese and biscuits with celery, cheese and pineapple, cheese and macaroni are only a few examples. In Yorkshire cheese is eaten with cake and apple pie; hence the Yorkshire saying 'An apple pie wi' owt tha' cheese is like a kiss wi' owt a squeeze!'

Most cheeses are made from cow's milk though a few are not; for example, from Norway comes a chocolate-coloured goat's milk cheese and from France comes Roquefort cheese made from sheep's milk. The details of cheese making vary for different cheeses, but the main features are similar, and we can use Cheddar cheese as an example (Fig. 33).

Cheese is a most nutritious food as you would expect from the fact that a pint of milk produces only about two ounces of cheese. You can see just what a rich source of nutrients cheese is if you look at Fig. 34. Cheese does not contain carbohydrate because the lactose in milk is converted into lactic acid during manufacture, but it contains every other class of nutrient. It is an excellent

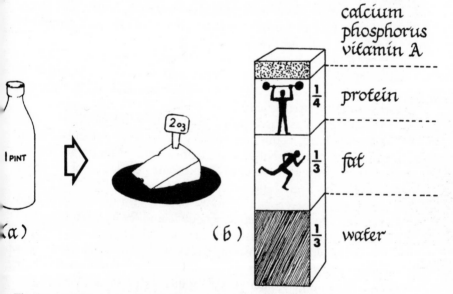

Fig. 34. (a) Cheese is a concentrated food, 2 oz. being produced from a pint of milk. (b) The nutrient content of cheese.

source of protein and calcium (Figs. 27 and 28) and also of fat and vitamin A.

Cheese is a highly concentrated food and so we only eat a little at a time. It is a valuable (and cheap) part of our diet, and is especially useful for packed meals and camping, when foods of small bulk are needed. It is more difficult to digest than milk and should be chewed well. Cooking does not improve its digestibility, and over-cooking makes it more difficult to digest because of over-coagulation of protein. Because cheese is so rich in protein and fat it is best eaten with a carbohydrate-rich food, such as bread or macaroni.

Eggs

Nowadays we think of an egg simply as food, but in the past it has been important in magic, witchcraft and fortune-telling among other things. For instance if you wanted to know your fortune in marriage, you let three drops of egg white fall from the point of an egg into water—on New Year's Eve! From the shape of the egg white in the water you could work out your marriage hopes with certainty! To-day we no longer have such faith in the powers of the egg, though we still have our chocolate eggs as a symbol of 'new birth' at Eastertime.

Even if we no longer believe in the magic powers of eggs, they still remain a valuable food. When we talk of eggs in connection with food, we nearly always mean hens' eggs, and so these are the sort we shall describe here.

A hen's egg has three parts; shell, white and yolk (Fig. 35). The shell is hard, being mainly calcium carbonate (chalk), and it protects the contents of the egg from harm. The colour of the shell varies from white to brown, and some people still believe that the colour has something to do with the quality of the egg. This is nonsense, however, as the colour depends on the breed of hen. In general heavy hens, such as Rhode Island Reds, lay brown eggs while lighter hens, such as Leghorns, lay white ones.

The hard shell contains tiny holes which allow gases to pass through; it is said to be *porous*. A fresh egg contains a small air pocket but as it gets older air passes into it and the air pocket gets bigger. Unfortunately bacteria pass into the egg with the air, and so eggs are liable to go bad on storage. The well-known 'bad

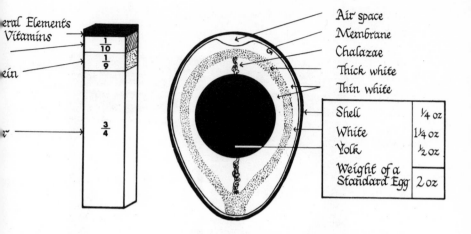

Fig. 35. The structure of a hen's egg and its nutrient content, excluding shell.

egg smell' of rotten eggs, due to hydrogen sulphide gas, is caused by action of bacteria on the sulphur in the egg protein.   When eggs are stored they should be put into a cool dry place with the blunt end (which contains the air pocket) at the top.   Because their shells are porous eggs absorb odours from other foods and so should be stored well away from anything with a strong smell.

Eggs may be preserved by sealing the tiny holes in the shell. This may be done by putting fresh eggs into water glass solution. Water glass deposits in the holes, sealing the shell so preventing the entry of air and bacteria into the egg.

Inside the shell is a thin membrane separating the shell and air pocket from the white.   Egg white is a colourless liquid being about seven-eighths water and one-eighth protein.   The main protein is *ovalbumin*, discussed on page 28.   In a fresh egg, the white surrounds the yolk and is divided into regions of thick and thin white.   Thus when you break a fresh egg into a dish you find that the yolk floats on top of the thick white and the egg spreads into a compact shape.   If the egg is old, the white is thinner, and the thin white flows outwards and the yolk sinks (Fig. 36).

The yolk of an egg is suspended in the white—being held in position by the *chalazae*—and is a rich source of nutrients.   It is about one-half water, one-third fat and one-quarter protein. The fat, like that of milk, is emulsified in water and so is easy to digest.   The colour of the yolk varies from light yellow to deep

4

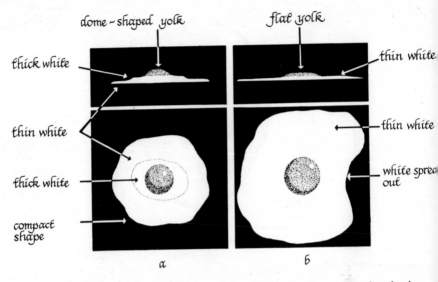

Fig. 36. The quality of an egg is shown by the way it spreads when broken onto a plate: (a) a good quality fresh egg; (b) a poor quality stale egg.

orange, and though you may prefer the deeper colour, do not make the mistake of thinking it is necessarily more nutritious than the lighter coloured yolk. Colour depends upon the diet of the hen.

A hen's egg has high nutritional value, as you might expect from the fact that it is designed as a complete food supply for an unborn chick growing inside it. Although it is not a complete food for humans it contains a good supply of body-building nutrients; good quality protein, and small amounts of calcium, phosphorus and sulphur. It is unfortunate that most of the mineral element content of an egg is in the shell which we cannot eat.

Eggs are not rich energy foods, but they do contain some fat in an easily digestible form. They also supply useful amounts of protective nutrients, especially iron and vitamins A and D; also some B vitamins.

Eggs are invaluable in cooking as you will see in Chapter 8.

Meat

Roast meat is still the basis of the traditional Sunday dinner in most homes in Great Britain. It is a good nutritional choice for

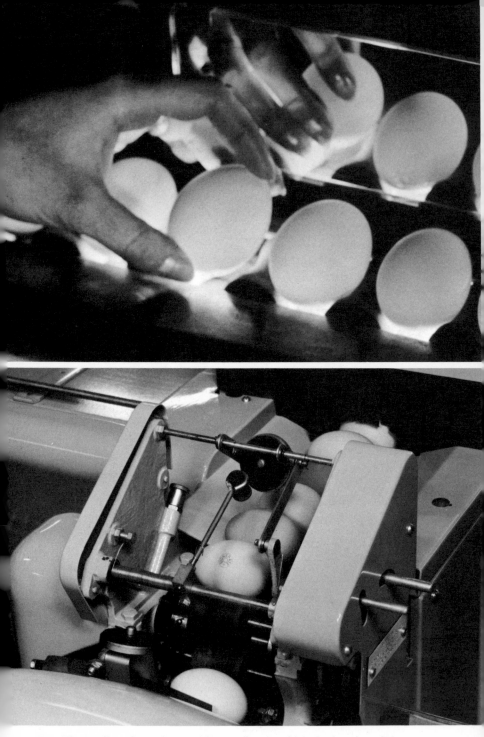

Top: The quality of eggs is tested by *candling* in which the interior of the egg is made visible by an intense light. *Bottom:* After candling, eggs are stamped and graded (foreground).

the main item in the meal, because it is not only a fine body-building food, but also a useful source of protective nutrients and energy.

When we talk about meat we usually mean lean meat, that is the flesh (muscular parts) of animals such as the bullock, pig and sheep which supply us with beef, pork and mutton respectively. We also eat the flesh of poultry, such as chicken and turkey, and of wild or 'game' birds, such as partridge and pheasant.

Muscle tissue is made up of tiny thread-like fibres which are held together by connective tissue to form bundles. Such tissue is about three-quarters water, one-quarter protein together with small amounts of fat, mineral elements and vitamins. The tenderness of lean flesh depends upon the nature of the muscle fibres and the amount of connective tissue. In old animals and in animals which have been very active there is a large amount of connective tissue, and this is tough and difficult to digest; also the muscle fibres are thick and tough. Therefore such meat must be carefully cooked if it is to become tender (see pages 135 and 142).

Meat is not cooked and eaten until it has been stored—or hung as it is called—for a time. This is because meat from freshly killed animals is tough, whereas after it has been hung it is more tender and has more flavour. The time for which meat is hung varies, but in the case of 'game' birds it is continued until the meat is 'high'; that is until it has started to decompose due to attack by micro-organisms.

Meat is mainly important as a body-building food, and it contains proteins of high nutritional value, the main one being *myosin*. Meat contains useful amounts of phosphorus but little calcium. The small amount of fat in lean meat is called 'invisible fat', because it is present in such minute particles in connective tissue that it cannot be seen. When you buy meat from the butchers you usually get some fat along with the lean. The amount of this visible fat, which is found just under the animal's skin, is much larger than the amount of invisible fat and explains why meat as eaten is a useful energy food.

The value of meat as a protective food is mainly due to the B vitamins and iron which it contains.

The organs of animals—such as liver and kidney—are also eaten, and these are called *offal*. Most offal has a higher nutritional value than flesh. Liver, for example, is one of the richest sources

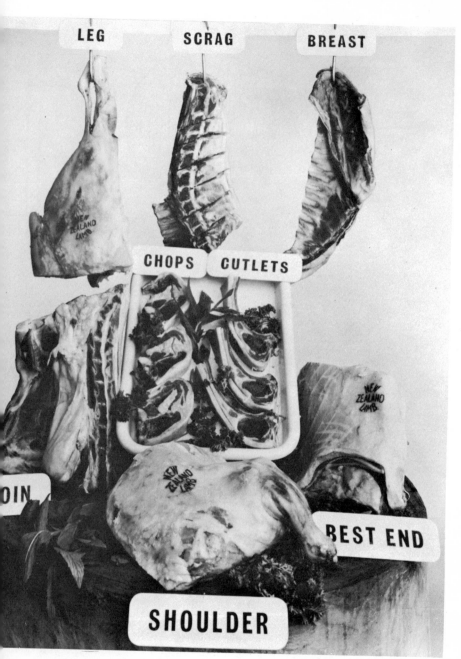

Different cuts of lamb.

85

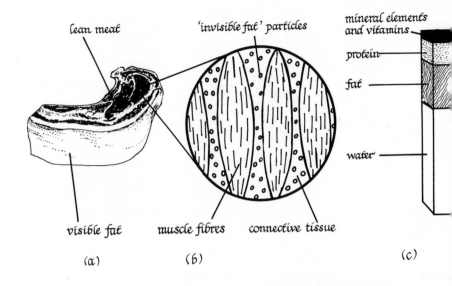

Fig. 37.   (a) A rib of lean beef showing (b) a magnified portion of the muscle tissue.   (c) The average nutrient content of beef.

of iron and contains valuable amounts of vitamin A in addition to the B vitamins.

Fish

Have you ever caught a large fish yourself, perhaps on one of your summer holidays? If you have, you will perhaps understand the thrill of hooking, playing and landing a great fish, such as a salmon. Salmon are most interesting fish; they are born in rivers where they spend their first two years. After this they swim down to the sea, where they spend another year. Every year afterwards they somehow manage to find their way through the great oceans back to the same river in which they were born. No matter what obstacles are put in their way, they never rest until they are back again in the quiet upper reaches of their own river. Here the female lays her eggs before she returns to the sea.

Salmon belong to the class of fish called *fat fish* as opposed to fish which contain little fat, which are called *white fish*. If you look at Fig. 38 you will see some examples of each type, and also their nutritional value.

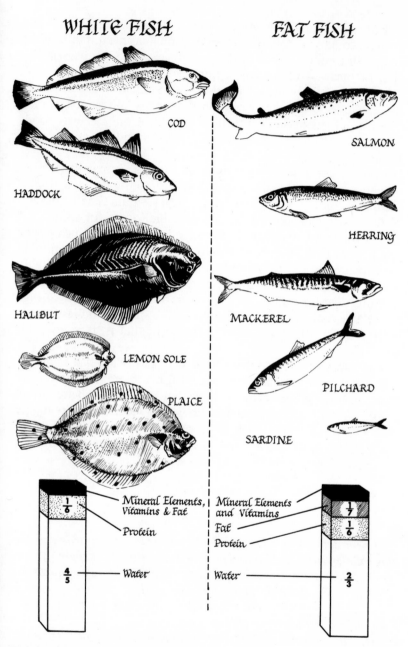

Fig. 38.   Some of the best known types of white fish and fat fish showing the
difference in their nutrient content.

Fish are mainly prized as fine body-building food. They contain roughly the same amount of protein as meat, that is about one-sixth to one-seventh of their total weight. Fish protein, like that of meat, is of high nutritional value. Fish are also good suppliers of phosphorus, though not of calcium unless the bones are eaten, as is the case with tinned sardines and tinned salmon.

White fish contain very little fat and are poor energy foods. Fat fish on the other hand contain more fat and are good energy foods.

Fish are useful protective foods, and sea fish in particular are a valuable source of iodine. Fish, with the notable exception of sardines, contain very little iron. Fish contain small amounts of the B vitamins and fat fish are valuable sources of vitamins A and D which are dissolved in the fat. Fish liver oils, such as cod and halibut liver oils, are especially rich sources of these vitamins.

Compared to meat, fish contain more waste matter, because we cannot eat parts such as the head, tail and fins. The flesh of fish is more digestible than that of meat because it has less tough connective tissue and the muscle fibres are shorter and less tough. All the fat in fish is dispersed in the flesh; that is, it is 'invisible fat'.

You can see from what we have said that white fish is just as valuable a food as meat, and that fat fish is more nutritious than meat. Most people seem to think that meat is the better food, but this is not true and we would do well to value fish more highly than we do. Fat fish, such as herring, have the double merit of being both cheap and nutritious. Also, fish need less cooking than meat and are more easily digested (see page 143).

SUMMARY

The most important body-building nutrients are proteins and the mineral elements calcium and phosphorus. Proteins supply us with amino acids and our diet must supply us with the essential amino acids (ten for children, eight for adults) that our bodies cannot make for themselves. On the whole, animal protein is of higher nutritive value than vegetable protein, because it contains all the essential amino acids whereas vegetable protein does not. To make the best use of protein, both animal and vegetable protein should be eaten together. Calcium and phosphorus are needed for bones and

teeth. One of the best sources of both these mineral elements is milk.

Milk is nearer to being a perfect food than any other. Although it is nine-tenths water, it contains high quality and easily digested protein (mainly casein), emulsified fat, milk sugar, vitamins (mainly A and B₂) as well as calcium and phosphorus. Unfortunately fresh milk contains bacteria, some of which may be harmful, and it will not keep without treatment. Pasteurized milk will keep for several days, sterilized milk for at least a week and usually much longer, while canned evaporated milk will keep as long as the can remains unopened.

Cheese, eggs, meat and fish are other good body-building foods. Cheese is made from milk, which is coagulated and the solid formed cut into small pieces to allow the liquid whey to drain off. Salt is added to the solid curd, which is dried, pressed and allowed to ripen. One pint of milk makes about two ounces of cheese, which is therefore a nutritious and concentrated food.

An egg has three parts; shell, white and yolk. The shell is the hard, porous covering which protects the white and yolk. The yolk is rich in nutrients and floats in the egg white, which is a watery liquid containing the protein ovalbumin. Eggs are good body-building foods containing high quality protein, calcium, phosphorus and sulphur. They also contain useful amounts of protective nutrients, mainly vitamins A and D, and iron.

Meat and fish contain one-sixth to one-seventh protein, which is of high nutritional value. They are also useful protective foods and liver in particular is a valuable source of iron while fish liver oils contain useful amounts of vitamins A and D. Fat fish and lean meat eaten with its covering of visible fat are also good energy foods. Meat which contains large amounts of connective tissue is tough, and needs careful cooking to make it more tender. Fish, on the other hand, contains less connective tissue and is less tough and so more easily digested.

6 Protective Foods and Water

We have already seen that we need fats and carbohydrates to supply us with energy and proteins for body-building. In addition to these nutrients, however, you will remember that our bodies require vitamins, mineral elements and water. Vitamins and mineral elements are needed for regulating the many chemical processes which go on inside our bodies. They help to protect us against disease and ill-health and they may be loosely termed *protective foods*. Mineral elements are also important for body-building processes of course, as we have seen in the last chapter. Last but not least there is water. Our bodies are almost two-thirds water, and since we lose several pints of it every day in various ways it is obvious that a regular supply of it is essential.

Vitamins

Vitamins are found in small amounts in many foods. Their presence in the diet is essential because, with a few exceptions, we are unable to make them for ourselves. Vitamins are necessary for growth, and if children do not get enough of them their growth may be slowed down. When a vitamin is missing from the diet, or is in very short supply, a disease known as a *deficiency disease* may occur. Deficiency diseases have been the cause of death and much suffering for many centuries, but they can now be prevented and cured by making sure that the diet contains sufficient vitamins.

Most vitamins are very complex chemicals. However, the exact chemical make-up of each one is now known and, with one exception, they can be prepared artificially by chemists. Before their chemical structures were determined the vitamins were known only by letters as vitamin A, vitamin B and so on, but when

their chemical structures became known they were given names. Some vitamins were found to be more complex than was at first supposed. Vitamin B, for example, has been shown to be not one but several vitamins and each of these has its own name. In some cases the names of the vitamins are so complicated that the letters originally given to the vitamins are still used.

Foods contain only very small quantities of vitamins, but these small amounts carry out some of the most important jobs in the body. The B vitamins, for example, form part of several enzyme systems which are essential for the maintenance of good health. The other vitamins are just as essential, though in some cases their exact job in the body is unknown.

Only very small amounts of vitamins are needed by our bodies, and the minute quantities present in foods are usually sufficient for our needs. They are, however, widely distributed amongst many kinds of food and to ensure that we get enough of *all* the vitamins, it is necessary for us to eat a varied diet. The vitamin content of a food can vary quite considerably. This is especially so with fruit and vegetables where the vitamin content depends, amongst other things, on freshness, variety and ripeness.

It is so important that we all receive enough vitamins that some foods have extra vitamins added to them. Flour, margarine and many baby foods and breakfast foods are fortified, or enriched with vitamins in this way.

The very small quantities of vitamins present in foods may be expressed as fractions of a gram or in special units called international units (i.u.). The size of an international unit varies from vitamin to vitamin. They were first used when the pure vitamins were not available and the exact weight of a vitamin in a food was not known. Nowadays the pure vitamins can be made and the quantities present in foods can be measured accurately. It is possible to say exactly what weight of a vitamin constitutes an international unit. For example, the international unit of vitamin A is now known to be $0 \cdot 0000003$ g. of the pure vitamin. This is a *very* minute quantity, and although an adult requires 5,000 i.u. of vitamin A per day, an ounce would be sufficient to last him for over fifty years! It would be quite useless to eat this quantity and then go without for fifty years, however, because our bodies are only able to store limited quantities of vitamin A. Regular and adequate quantities of vitamins are required and this is especially so for the water-soluble vitamins, such as vitamin C and the B

vitamins. Our bodies are unable to build up a reserve of these, and any excess over immediate requirements is excreted in the urine.

You may be surprised that such small quantities of vitamins are so important that our bodies are unable to carry on without them. In some ways vitamins are to our bodies what lubricating oil is to a machine. Only small amounts of oil are required by a machine but these small amounts are necessary if it is to run smoothly. Without oil the machine will carry on for a while, but it will run less and less smoothly and become less and less efficient. In time the machine will be unable to continue without oil and it will stop. The action of vitamins in our bodies is much like this. If our food contains less vitamins than we need we can still carry on, but our bodies are not able to make the most efficient use of our food, and in time the shortage will show itself as a deficiency disease. In extreme cases of vitamin deficiency death may result.

The more important vitamins are discussed below. Several others are known but they are widely distributed in foods and there is no danger of a shortage of them.

Vitamin A. Vitamin A is a pale-yellow solid which dissolves easily in fats and oils, but not in water.

The most important sources of vitamin A in the diet are green vegetables and dairy products. Green vegetables do not contain vitamin A as such, however. They contain substances known as *carotenes*, which are easily converted by our bodies—and also by animals such as sheep and cows—into vitamin A. Carotenes are brightly coloured, and are responsible for the colour of carrots, the yellow colour of unripe tomatoes and butter and the creamy colour of cream. When vegetables are eaten our bodies are unable to convert all the carotenes to vitamin A. For this reason animal sources of the vitamin are much more effective in the diet than vegetable sources.

The vitamin A content of dairy products such as milk, butter and cheese depends upon the amount of carotenes in the food eaten by the cow. For this reason milk may be richer in vitamin A during the summer—when cows are able to feed on fresh grass —than in winter when only hay and animal feeding-stuffs are available. Vitamin A is added to many proprietary cattle foods, however, and in this case as much of the vitamin may be present in winter milk as in summer milk.

92

As butter and cheese are made from milk, the vitamin A from milk is present in these foods. At one time margarine contained little or no vitamin A, but nowadays margarine manufacturers must add vitamin A to it. Margarine now contains at least as much vitamin A as is present in butter.

Other good sources of vitamin A are eggs and liver. Fish liver oils are particularly rich in the vitamin and may be used to supplement the dietary sources.

Vitamin A is necessary for growth and so it is very important that babies and young children receive enough of it. Shortage in infancy during the formation of teeth may produce poor teeth, and even after the teeth have been formed lack of vitamin A may affect the enamel. A condition known as *night-blindness* may arise as a result of vitamin A shortage. Sufferers from this find it difficult to see in poor light. A severe deficiency of vitamin A may cause an eye disease which may ultimately lead to blindness. Dryness of the skin and a lower resistance to infection are also caused by a shortage of vitamin A.

The B group of vitamins. Several vitamins which have similar jobs to do in the body, and which are often found in the same foods, are included in the B group of vitamins. The B vitamins form a part of several enzyme systems in the body and they help to release the energy from food. They are, in fact, *co-enzymes*, that is substances which assist enzymes to carry out their work. The B vitamins dissolve in water, and if more is eaten than the body requires it is excreted in the urine. The more important members of the B group of vitamins are *thiamine* (which is also called vitamin B_1), *riboflavin* (also called vitamin B_2) and *nicotinamide*.

The co-enzymes which our bodies make from the B vitamins are used in releasing the energy from the carbohydrates in our food. Because the amount of carbohydrate eaten varies from person to person it is difficult to say with certainty how much B vitamins we need. A very small quantity is enough, however, and even a Billy Bunter with a huge appetite would only need one-fiftieth of a gram each day.

Thiamine or vitamin B_1. Thiamine is a white water-soluble solid. It is made artificially on quite a large scale for adding to white flour to replace the thiamine which is lost during milling.

Thiamine is found in many foodstuffs. The main sources in a normal diet are bread, potatoes, meat and milk. Because it dissolves easily in water, as much as half the thiamine present in vegetables may be lost when they are boiled.

Deficiency of thiamine produces a check in the growth of children together with a loss of appetite and fatigue. Severe shortage can cause the disease *beriberi*.

Beriberi is almost unknown in this country, but it causes much suffering in Far Eastern countries where the standard of living is very low. In these countries the main article of diet is polished rice which contains little or no thiamine. Polished rice is made by removing from rice the husk and an outer layer or membrane called the silverskin. Both husk and silverskin contain appreciable quantities of thiamine. They are removed to improve the appearance of the rice—and because the husk is hard and difficult to digest.

You may think it strange that people should suffer as a result of the deliberate removal of a nutrient from a food. It is, indeed, unfortunate that this should be so. A similar situation exists in Western countries where most of the thiamine present in wheat is lost in the production of white flour. To counteract this, thiamine is added to all flour except wholemeal flour, and it provides about one-quarter of all the thiamine in an average diet.

Riboflavin or vitamin B₂. Riboflavin is a yellow crystalline substance which is found in many plant and animal tissues. It is only slightly soluble in water, and so not much is lost when food is boiled. It is, however, sensitive to light and three-quarters of the riboflavin in milk may be destroyed when milk is allowed to stand in direct sunlight for three hours. This is a good reason for not leaving milk on the doorstep any longer than is absolutely necessary! Riboflavin is found in quite a large number of foods. Milk, meat, potatoes, cereals and eggs are the main sources in the average diet.

A shortage of riboflavin causes a check in the growth of children, and in addition sores may develop.

Nicotinic acid and nicotinamide. Nicotinic acid and nicotinamide are both white crystalline solids. Nicotinic acid was first made—long before it was known to be a vitamin—from nicotine which is

94

present in tobacco. In food, however, it is ⟨...⟩
nicotine nor is it formed during tobacco smoking⟨...⟩
is called *niacin* in the United States because it was fe⟨...⟩
people would assume that nicotine absorbed during sm⟨...⟩
serve as a source of the vitamin. Large quantities of ⟨...⟩
acid are now made for addition to white flour to replace tha⟨...⟩
during milling.

Nicotinic acid was first found in food about fifty years ago,
when it was discovered in rice polishings. Plants contain the
vitamin as nicotinic acid and animal tissues contain it as nicotinamide. Both substances are similar and equally active as vitamins, because nicotinic acid is converted into nicotinamide by our
bodies when we eat it. Meat, bread and potatoes are the main
sources of them both in the diet.

A deficiency of nicotinic acid causes a check in the growth of
children and, if severe, the disease *pellagra*. Pellagra was known
to be associated with a low standard of living for many years before
vitamins were discovered. Poor people in the Southern States of
America—who lived mainly on maize—suffered greatly from
pellagra in former times. Maize contains only small amounts of
nicotinic acid, and only small amounts of the amino acid *trypto-
phan*, which our bodies can convert to nicotinamide.

Other B vitamins. Other members of the B group of vitamins are
also known, but they are not as important as those dealt with
above. Pyridoxine (or vitamin B_6), pantothenic acid and biotin
are some of these. They are found in foods with the other B
vitamins and there is no danger of a shortage of them. Vitamin
B_{12}, another member of the group, is particularly interesting because it contains a mineral element—cobalt. It is found in milk,
meat and especially liver. In these foods it is combined with
protein and is set free during digestion. People in normal health
obtain adequate amounts of vitamin B_{12} from their food. Some
people are unable to release the vitamin from its combination
with protein, however, and they suffer from a condition known as
pernicious anaemia. This is a severe form of anaemia which does
not improve when treated in the same way as ordinary anaemia.
By taking vitamin B_{12}, however, the disease may be kept in check.

Ascorbic acid or vitamin C. This is a white, sharp-tasting solid
which dissolves easily in water. It occurs mainly in fruits and

...ables. Blackcurrants and strawberries are particularly rich in the vitamin but unfortunately many popular eating apples, pears and plums contain only small amounts. Green vegetables, potatoes and fresh fruit supply most of the vitamin C in our diet.

The amount of vitamin C present in vegetables is greatest in the periods of active growth in spring and early summer. Storage decreases the ascorbic acid content and old potatoes contain much less than new potatoes. Potatoes are a very valuable source of vitamin C, although weight for weight they contain less of the vitamin than green vegetables. A normal serving of boiled new potatoes provides about 90% of the recommended daily intake of vitamin C.

As much as 75% of the vitamin C contained in green vegetables may be lost when they are cooked. This loss can be avoided by eating green vegetables raw in salads, but the amount which can be eaten in this way is small. Even allowing for losses in cooking, larger quantities of vitamin C are obtained from a normal serving of cabbage than from a normal serving of lettuce. Five times as much vitamin C is obtainable from 4 oz. of cooked cabbage as from 1 oz.—which is about as much as one normally eats—of raw lettuce. Enough vitamin C to last a whole day is contained in 1 oz. of raw cabbage, which is a much better source of the vitamin than lettuce.

Cow's milk contains only about one-third as much vitamin C as human milk, and some of this is destroyed during pasteurization. Exposure of milk to sunlight also destroys some of the vitamin C. It is important that babies, and particularly those fed on cow's milk which has been boiled, should be given extra vitamin C. Rose-hip syrup or concentrated orange or black-current juice can be used for this purpose. When babies progress to a mixed diet there is less need for such supplements, and at two years of age the normal diet should provide sufficient vitamin C.

Foods—such as yeast, egg-yolk, meats and cereals—which are rich in B vitamins, usually contain little or no vitamin C.

A shortage of vitamin C in the diet prevents children growing properly. Severe deficiency may cause the disease *scurvy*, which has been known for hundreds of years and was at one time very common in Europe in the winter months when fresh food was short. It was especially troublesome to sailors who were unable to get fresh food. The cause of the disease was not known, nor any way of curing it though many strange methods were tried.

One British admiral tried to cure his sailors of scurvy by burying them in boxes of earth normally used for growing vegetables for salads!

During the eighteenth century it became clear that scurvy could be prevented and cured by eating fruits and vegetables or their juices. Once this was realised lemon juice was carried by ships for use in preventing scurvy. Unfortunately, however, outbreaks of scurvy still occurred for a very long time after it was known that fruit juice would prevent it. During the Crimean War in the middle of the last century more British soldiers died from scurvy than were killed in action. This great loss of life could have been prevented, for ample supplies of fruit juice had been sent from England, but it was never distributed to the troops. The Crimean War is now mainly remembered for the gallant but disastrous charge of the Light Brigade, but the great loss of life from scurvy was undoubtedly more tragic. Even during the 1914–18 war scurvy caused much suffering amongst besieged British troops in Turkey. Happily the disease is fairly uncommon in this country at the present time.

A shortage of vitamin C not severe enough to cause scurvy may make the mouth and gums easily infected and slow down the rate at which broken bones and wounds heal. Some people think that colds last longer if the body is not getting enough vitamin C.

Vitamin D. Naturally occurring vitamin D is a white solid which dissolves in oils and fats but not in water. It is not present in many foods and is found only in foods of animal origin. Fish liver oils are the most important source. Eggs and dairy products also contain some. Because it is found in only a few foods there is more danger of a shortage of vitamin D than of any other vitamin. For this reason synthetic vitamin D is now added to all table margarine made in this country, and also to many baby foods. Margarine contains about five times as much vitamin D as butter and it provides about one third of the vitamin D in the average diet.

Vitamin D is necessary for the proper formation of bones, and a baby or child who does not receive enough will suffer from the disease called *rickets*. At one time rickets was very common in this country, but as a result of better feeding it is now almost unknown. Rickets can be treated by exposure to sunlight or any other source of ultra-violet light (e.g. a sun-lamp). This is

because vitamin D is formed in the skin under the influence of ultra-violet light.

Vitamin D is also essential for healthy teeth. Not only does it help to form good teeth, but it also helps to prevent infection of existing teeth. It is needed by our bodies before proper use can be made of the calcium and phosphorus in our food. This explains why a shortage of vitamin D has such a bad effect on the bones and teeth.

Because vitamin D is so important for the formation of strong bones and healthy teeth it is vital that children should receive enough of it. Young children should take fish liver oil or a vitamin D concentrate regularly.

Mineral Elements as Protective Foods

We have already seen in Chapter 5 that mineral elements play a most important part in building up our bodies. They are also, however, important as protective foods. Calcium, sodium, iron and iodine are the most important mineral elements from this point of view, but others are also involved in the many reactions taking place in our bodies. Mineral elements which have this protective function are found as constituents of cells or in the body fluids. Most of them are adequately provided by a well-balanced diet, but shortage of iron and calcium may easily occur.

Sodium and chlorine. All the body fluids contain sodium and chlorine in the form of sodium chloride. Our bodies are continually losing salt in urine and perspiration. The concentration of salt in the body fluids must be maintained at a certain level, and since there is no way of controlling the loss of salt from the body, all the salt lost must be replaced. If our food did not contain enough salt to replace that lost, our bodies would soon give an alarm signal in the form of painful cramps.

The fact that salt is essential for health has been realised for thousands of years. In countries where salt is scarce it is prized and has been used as money. Salt was in short supply in this country in bygone days and the Roman forces of occupation were paid part of their wages in salt. Indeed this is the origin of our modern word 'salary' which means literally salt money. As little as thirty years ago salt was legal tender in Ethiopia even for paying taxes and fines!

The amount of salt lost from the body can vary considerably because some people perspire more than others. Heavy manual workers need more salt than office workers, for example, because they are likely to lose more salt in perspiration. This is true also of people who live in hot countries. In this country about 4 g. of salt is needed daily by an adult following a normal occupation. Salt is present in most foods but the actual quantities obtained from food are not important. Most people get more than enough from the salt used in cooking and as a condiment. Salt is also used by our bodies for making the hydrochloric acid present in the gastric juice. An excess of salt does no harm because it is removed from the body by the kidneys and is excreted in the urine.

Iron. The body of an adult contains about 4 g. of iron—roughly the amount in a 3-inch nail. It is a most important mineral element because it enables us to take the oxygen from the air and use it in the oxidation processes involved in releasing energy from food. Iron is an essential part of the compound *haemoglobin* which makes red blood cells red. The job of the red blood cells is to carry oxygen from the lungs to the tissues where it is needed for releasing the energy from sugars. Every cell in the body must be supplied with oxygen and if the number of red cells in our blood were to fall below a certain level it would be difficult for the blood to supply the tissues with enough oxygen. People in this condition are said to be *anaemic* and they are usually given iron tablets to assist in making new red blood cells.

Haemoglobin combines with oxygen in our lungs and carries it to every part of our bodies, giving up its oxygen to the cells requiring it. Each molecule of haemoglobin can combine with one molecule of oxygen, and when it does so it becomes brighter red in colour. When it gives up the oxygen it changes back to a much duller, purplish red. The bluish veins on our wrists or on the backs of our hands contain blood that has given up its oxygen to the tissues. It is being pumped back up our arms to the lungs where it will pick up a further supply of oxygen.

Red blood cells do not last for ever but have a life of about four months. The body is very thrifty with the iron contained in the old red blood cells, however, and re-uses most of it to make new ones. Some additional iron is needed, and this is especially so when the volume of blood is increasing, that is when a child is growing. It is obviously important to have sufficient iron in

our food and it is therefore most unfortunate that it is one of the mineral elements which may be lacking in an average diet. To try to prevent this, iron is now added to all flour in this country except wholemeal flour. Bread and flour provide about a quarter of the iron in an average diet, the other main suppliers being meat and vegetables.

Iodine. Iodine is another mineral element which is essential to the proper functioning of our bodies. The iodine in our food is transported to a small gland—called the thyroid gland—at the base of the throat. It is used to make a compound called *thyroxine*.

If enough iodine is not obtained from food or drinking-water a condition known as *goitre* may result. In this disease the thyroid gland becomes enlarged and is visible as a large swelling or 'growth' at the base of the throat. Goitre is sometimes called 'Derbyshire neck' because it was at one time common in Derbyshire. Because of the swelling—which can be large and unsightly—goitre is usually regarded as a disfiguring ailment. This has not always been the case, however, and in eighteenth-century France a lady's beauty was thought to be enhanced by the possession of a small goitre!

Thyroxine has many jobs to do in the body, but one of its most important tasks is to control the rate at which the body burns up food and converts it into energy. When we are working hard the reactions going on inside our bodies must be speeded up to provide us with enough energy. Even when we are resting or sleeping our internal body processes are still working and we still use up energy, but at a reduced rate. We may say that our bodies are 'ticking-over' when we are asleep and ready to start work again when required. The rate of tick-over—known by the rather grand name of *basal metabolic rate*—is higher than usual in people with an active thyroid gland which makes a lot of thyroxine. Such people are usually restless, active people. They may eat a lot and still stay thin because their food is burned up comparatively quickly by their bodies and is not converted to body fat. Other people, with less active thyroid glands which make a smaller quantity of thyroxine, are slower and less energetic and they become fat more easily.

Obviously iodine is very important in the body and a deficiency of it can have unpleasant results. Fortunately the amounts

required are very small—one-tenth of an ounce of iodine would be sufficient to last for a lifetime. Sea foods are the best sources of iodine in the diet. Fish is an excellent source and it provides about one quarter of the iodine in an average diet. Cod liver oil is the richest natural source.

Seaweed contains valuable amounts of iodine, which it collects from the sea water. Seaweed is not very widely eaten, but in some parts of the country it is regarded as a delicacy. In South Wales, for example, cooked seaweed—known as laver bread—has been popular for many years. Even sponges accumulate iodine from sea water although no one has yet gone so far as to eat them! Centuries ago, however, before anything was known about the causes of goitre the ancient Chinese successfully treated the condition with 'ashes of sponges'.

Where the iodine content of the diet is likely to be small the use of iodized salt is a useful precaution. This contains 1 part of potassium iodide to about 40,000 parts of salt. If the diet contains more iodine than is required the excess is excreted in the urine.

Calcium. Most of the calcium in our food is used, as we saw in Chapter 5, for forming bones and teeth. A small amount of calcium circulates in the blood, which conveys it to and from the bones and teeth. The concentration of calcium in the blood is kept constant, and if there is not enough calcium in our food our bones will be slowly *decalcified*, that is the calcium will be removed from them. The calcium in the bloodstream helps the blood to clot properly and so prevents excessive bleeding from cuts. It also plays a part in the working of nerves and muscles.

Fruits and Vegetables as Sources of Protective Nutrients

Fruits and vegetables are of value as providers of vitamins and mineral elements, though they supply carbohydrates and proteins as well. In general it may be said that fruits are less important than vegetables as a source of vitamins and minerals. In fact fruits may almost be neglected as a source of mineral elements. They do, however, supply valuable amounts of vitamin C, and in an average diet about one-third of this vitamin is supplied by fruits. The Calorie value of most fruits is small, and this is the main attraction of fruit to some people. Fruit is almost always included in

'slimming diets' because it provides vitamin C without adding greatly to the Calorie value of the diet. In this way fruit makes up for the reduced vitamin C intake from potatoes which are usually absent from slimming diets.

Vegetables provide carbohydrates, proteins and protective nutrients in the diet. Green vegetables are good sources of vitamin A and vitamin C, though not all of the former may be absorbed by the body. Carrots, also, are rich in vitamin A. The most important vegetable, from a nutritional point of view, is undoubtedly the potato because such large quantities of these are eaten. They supply about 10% of the iron, 15% of the nicotinic acid and thiamine and 35% of the vitamin C in an average diet. Vegetables as a whole provide over half the vitamin C and about 20% of the iron and B vitamins in an average diet.

Water

All living things—from the simplest bacteria to the giant oak tree—are made up largely of water and are constantly losing water. As we have seen, our bodies are two-thirds water, and we lose water in our breath, in perspiration and in urine. Obviously the water lost from our bodies must be replaced, or in time we would completely dry up. It is possible for us to live for fairly long periods without food, because our bodies can use up reserves of fat. Although we would get thinner and feel very hungry, we would still be getting fed while these food reserves lasted. No one can go for very long without water, however, because our bodies—unlike the camel's—do not have a reserve supply.

The water in our bodies acts as a form of water transport. Our blood circulation system—which is mainly composed of water—can be likened to a network of canals, which carries food to the tissues and brings back waste materials, such as carbon dioxide and urea. The carbon dioxide is removed from the blood by the lungs and it is replaced by a supply of oxygen. The urea and excess water in the blood are removed by the kidneys and in this way the blood is 'reconditioned' to carry out its work again. All the tissues of the body are bathed in a watery fluid, and this is regularly renewed by the blood.

The quantity of water a person drinks is largely determined by personal preference. It is impossible to drink too much, however,

because any excess over our needs is promptly removed from the blood by the kidneys and excreted in the urine.

The water we drink is not pure because it contains small quantities of dissolved solids and gases. Oxygen, nitrogen and carbon dioxide are picked up when the water falls as rain through the air. In industrial areas sulphur dioxide may also be picked up in the same way. When rain water percolates through the ground it dissolves small quantities of mineral salts—chiefly the sulphates and bicarbonates of calcium and magnesium. When calcium and magnesium compounds are present in water they make it difficult to obtain a lather with soap. Such water is said to be 'hard'. Hard water makes good drinking water because of the dissolved calcium it contains but the amount of calcium our bodies get in this way is quite small. By removing the mineral salts which cause hardness, it is possible to 'soften' hard water so that it will easily form a lather with soap.

Natural water contains dissolved oxygen and also material derived from vegetation and animals. Polluted water supplies may be the cause of diseases such as typhoid fever, cholera and jaundice and in order to purify drinking water it is often treated before use by adding about 1 part of chlorine to 2,000,000 parts of the water. This kills most of the bacteria, but the chlorine is present in such small amounts that it cannot be tasted (see page 107).

The presence of small amounts of *fluorine* salts in drinking water is beneficial because it helps to prevent teeth from decaying. The effect is most noticeable in children under eight years of age. Only about 1 part of fluorine salt in 1,000,000 parts of water is required. In some parts of Britain—where the concentration of fluorine in the water is lower than this—fluorine salts are added to the water to help prevent dental decay.

Beverages. Many people drink little or no water as such but rely on tea, coffee and other drinks to quench their thirst. Our bodies are able to extract the water from these drinks quite efficiently and they serve almost as well as pure water. Tea and coffee have practically no nutritional value in themselves, but the sugar and milk with which they are usually drunk has food value.

The tea plant is an evergreen shrub which grows in warm countries. The choicest leaves are picked and after drying in the sun they are allowed to ferment. During this process they become reddish-brown in colour and the familiar tea flavour develops.

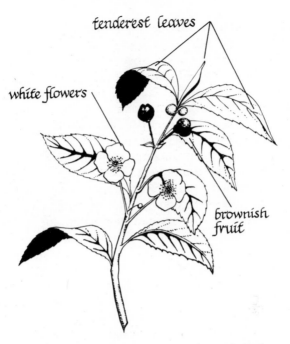

image labels:
tenderest leaves
white flowers
brownish fruit

Fig. 39.   A branch of the tea shrub, showing the tenderest leaves, which are the only ones used for making good quality tea.

The leaves are then dried in a current of hot air which destroys the enzymes and so prevents further fermentation.   The most important ingredients of tea are *caffeine* and *tannin*.   Caffeine has a mild stimulating or pick-me-up action and this is one reason why tea is such a popular drink.   Tannin has a bitter taste and a well-made cup of tea should not contain much of it.

Both caffeine and tannin are extracted from tea leaves by hot water, but tannin is extracted more slowly than caffeine.   When tea is allowed to stand in the teapot, more and more tannin is extracted and the tea becomes bitter.   This is why a second cup of tea is never as nice as the first.   As well as tannin and caffeine, tea contains small amounts of flavouring materials called *essential oils*.   It is the essential oils which give high-grade tea its pleasing aroma and delicate taste.

The coffee plant, like the tea plant, is an evergreen shrub which is cultivated in many tropical countries, especially Brazil.   The fruit looks like a cherry and contains two seeds or beans enclosed in a tough skin (see page 105).   The beans are dried in air and the

An African woman picking coffee 'cherries' from mature coffee bushes.

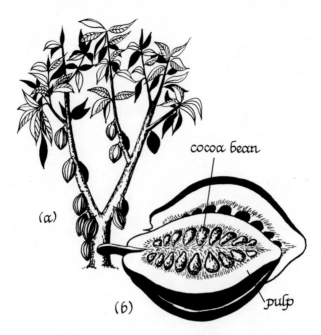

cocoa bean

pulp

(a)

(b)

Fig. 40.　(a) A cocoa tree and (b) a cocoa pod.

skin or husk is removed by rolling.　The caffeine content of coffee beans is only about one-third that of tea.　They also contain tannin and a complex mixture of essential oils and other compounds which provide the characteristic coffee flavour.　As is well known, coffee beans are roasted and ground before use.　Ground coffee rapidly loses its flavour if it is allowed to stand in air, and so it should always be stored in an airtight container.　The aim of good coffee-making is to extract the maximum amount of flavouring matter and caffeine, and the minimum amount of tannin. Coffee is expensive and chicory—which adds to the colour and the flavour—is often mixed with it to make it cheaper.

Cocoa trees are grown in many tropical countries, and are somewhat like apple trees both in size and shape.　Cocoa beans— from which both cocoa and chocolate are made—grow in large egg-shaped pods (Fig. 40).　After harvesting, the pods are split open and the beans scraped out.　They are fermented for several days and dried.　In making cocoa (and chocolate) the beans are first roasted, and it is this process which causes the well-known chocolate flavour and aroma to develop.　After roasting, the beans are broken into small pieces called *nibs* and ground.

106

Grinding turns the nibs into a thick brown liquid which sets into a fatty solid. Some of the fat, which is called *cocoa butter*, is squeezed out, and the solid left is turned into cocoa powder by careful grinding and sieving.

Unlike tea and coffee, cocoa powder is a nutritious food and contains roughly a fifth protein, a quarter fat and a third carbo-hydrate. In addition it contains small amounts of iron, calcium, vitamin A and the B vitamins. When cocoa is drunk as a beverage it is mixed with hot milk (or water), and is a valuable food. It also has a mild pick-me-up action because it contains small amounts of the stimulant *theobromine*.

Water from food. Almost all the solid food we eat contains quite a lot of water. There is more water in some fruits and vegeta-bles than there is in milk. Lettuce, for example, contains about 97% water compared with about 87% in milk. The water con-tent of food which we normally regard as 'dry' food can also be substantial—bread contains about 40% water and eggs about 70%. Most people get between a pint and a pint and a half of water a day from 'solid' food, and their bodies make use of this in exactly the same way as water from drinks.

A natural reservoir. Even such clean-looking water as this needs careful treatment before it is fit for drinking.

SUMMARY

Vitamins, mineral elements and water are necessary for the maintenance of good health. The sources and functions of these are summarized in the following table.

VITAMINS

Name	Main Sources	Functions in the body and effect of shortage
Vitamin A	Green vegetables, milk, dairy products, margarine, fish liver oil	Necessary for healthy skin and teeth and also for normal growth and development. Deficiency will slow down growth and may lead to disorders of the skin, lowered resistance to infection and disturbances of vision such as night blindness.
The B Vitamins: Thiamine, Riboflavin, Nicotinic Acid, Nicotin-amide	Bread and flour, meat, milk, potatoes, yeast extract	Function as co-enzymes in many of the reactions involved in making use of food. Shortage causes loss of appetite, slows growth and development and impairs general health. Severe deficiency may lead to a deficiency disease such as pellagra or beriberi.
Vitamin C (Ascorbic Acid)	Green vegetables, fruits, potatoes, blackcurrant syrup, rosehip syrup	Necessary for the proper formation of teeth, bones and blood vessels. Shortage causes a check in the growth of children and if prolonged may lead to the disease scurvy.
Vitamin D	Margarine, butter, milk, fish liver oils, fat fish	Necessary for the formation of strong bones and teeth. A shortage may cause rickets and possibly dental decay.

MINERAL ELEMENTS AND WATER

Name	Main Sources	Functions in the body and effect of shortage
Sodium	Widely distributed in foods. Sodium chloride is extensively used in cooking and as a condiment	Sodium chloride is present in all the body fluids, and is used for making hydrochloric acid present in gastric juices. Shortage causes cramp.
Iron	Bread, flour, meat, liver, potatoes, eggs	Used by the body to make haemoglobin, which is present in the red blood cells. Shortage causes anaemia.
Iodine	Drinking water, fish, fish liver oil, iodized salt, milk, and cereals	The body uses iodine to make thyroxine which regulates the rate at which the body functions. Absence or shortage causes goitre.
Calcium	Bread, flour, milk, and cheese	Used for the formation of bones and teeth and is also present in the blood. Shortage severely affects the bones, which become soft and weak. It is also necessary for the proper clotting of the blood and the normal functioning of the muscles.
Water	Drinking water, tea, coffee, milk, vegetables, fruits and most foods	Water is the medium in which the body's thousand and one reactions occur. It is used for transporting nutrients and waste materials to and from the tissues. The body cannot tolerate a shortage of water for any length of time.

7 Meal Planning and a Balanced Diet

We have seen that food supplies us with essential nutrients for doing three things; for giving us energy, for body-building, and for control of body processes. We have also seen in the last three chapters which foods carry out these functions. You will no doubt be able to think of some foods which carry out all three of these functions in the body. Milk, for example, is one of the most valuable foods in our diet for it contains every class of nutrient. Yet you would not remain healthy very long if your diet consisted of nothing but milk, for though it contains both mineral elements and vitamins, it contains very little *iron* and *vitamin D*.

In other words milk is not a *perfect* food because it does not contain all the essential nutrients in the proportions needed by our bodies. There is no single food known which is a perfect food, and it follows that a satisfactory diet must be based not on one, but on several foods.

When we talk of a satisfactory diet we mean one that will supply us with all our needs. We often call this a *balanced diet*; that is one which supplies us with *all* the essential nutrients and which contains them in the *correct proportions* for our needs.

There are lots of different ways of making a balanced diet, and that is why planning diets is so interesting. It is possible to work out balanced diets based on only a few foods. For instance, a diet based on three foods—milk, wholemeal bread and green vegetables—would be satisfactory from a nutritional point of view, though it would not be very exciting! There is also the danger that if we try to use only a few foods the diet will not be balanced. For example, in the last century the diet of the poorer people of Ireland was based mainly on a single food—the potato. Potatoes are a valuable food, but a diet based on them will be a mainly

110

starchy diet and though it might provide enough Calories it would not provide enough of some other nutrients. In general, although it is *possible* to plan balanced diets based on only a few foods, it is much better to use as wide a variety of foods as possible.

In planning a diet, we must think of the needs of the person who is going to live on it. It is fairly obvious, for example, that a diet which suits a farm worker would be disastrous for a baby! In Great Britain we have as a guide a set of recommended allowances of each nutrient for various types of people. If you turn back to Fig. 18 on page 44 you will see how daily Calorie allowances vary with occupation. Calorie allowances also vary according to whether a person is slim or fat, whether they are old or young and so on. Protein allowances are calculated on the basis of our Calorie needs, and very roughly we can say that in a balanced diet protein should supply adults with at least 11% of their Calories. Thus if their daily Calorie allowance is 3,000 Calories, then they should eat enough protein to provide them with at least 330 Calories. As the Calorie value of protein is 4 Cal./g., the protein allowance in this case would be not less then 82 g. For young people, at least 14% of the Calorie intake should be supplied by protein.

There is a recommended allowance for each essential nutrient, and you will be able to get some idea of some of these for a typical family from Fig. 41.

Foods and a Balanced Diet

It is no good knowing how much of each nutrient we should have for good health unless we also know which foods in the diet supply us with particular nutrients. For example, you cannot plan a diet that will supply 90 g. of protein daily as recommended for an active male worker, unless you know how much protein each food in the diet supplies. To know this we can use *food tables*, which tell us the nutrient content of every food. If you look at Fig. 27 on page 69 you will soon be able to plan a daily diet that will contain 90 g. of protein.

A diet is, of course, made up of meals, and so by using food tables, we can calculate exactly how much of each nutrient we obtain from a meal. At this point you may be thinking that meal planning seems rather like an unpleasant exercise in arithmetic!

Calories	3000	2500	2000	1000
g. Protein	90	70	70	40
g. Calcium	0·8	0·8	1	1
g. Iron	0·012	0·012	0·01	0·006
g. Vitamin C	0·02	0·02	0·02	0·01
	Father, fairly active	Mother, active housewife	Child, 7-10 years old	Baby, not yet 1 year old

Fig. 41.   Recommended daily allowances of some nutrients for members of a typical family.

In case you have got this impression, it should be said that normally it is quite unnecessary to calculate the exact nutrient content of each meal.   It is enough if you know the main nutrients in each food, so that you can check if a meal contains roughly balanced amounts of nutrients.   For example, Fig. 42 shows you the portions of various foods that supply a hundred Calories, and you can see at a glance which of these foods you should include in a meal planned to give plenty of energy.   Butter, sugar, chocolate and cheese are concentrated sources of Calories, while tomatoes, oranges and bananas are poor sources.

We can now go on to consider how to plan a balanced and varied diet in terms of meals.   Before we do this we must point out that sometimes it *is* necessary to calculate the nutrient content of each meal.   For example, if you have tried to slim you will know that you have to 'count each Calorie' if you really want to get slimmer. Also, in hospitals it is often necessary to give patients special diets, and this may involve exact calculation of its nutrient content.

Fig. 42.   Portions of food that supply
100 Calories.

General Principles of Meal Planning

In planning an attractive balanced meal the following general principles should be followed. The meal should contain foods which are rich in protein and foods which are rich in protective nutrients, that is mineral elements and vitamins. Once these requirements have been met, then enough energy-giving food should be included to satisfy the apetite. In brief, 'Count the body-building and protective foods and the Calories will look after themselves!' The meal should also include enough different foods to make it interesting, and these should be cooked and served so as to make the various dishes as attractive as possible.

The information given in the table on page 114 should be a help in planning meals, though care is needed in using it. The indication of nutritional value given refers to the amount in one unit of food. It does not take into account the amount of the food that is normally eaten. Thus an ounce of milk has less body-building value than an ounce of cheese, yet because we usually consume large amounts of milk but only small amounts of cheese, milk makes a greater contribution to body-building than cheese.

The first three foods in the table—milk, potatoes and bread— are staple foods in British diets, and because large amounts of them are eaten they supply a large proportion of the nutrients in our diet. Thus between them they provide about two-fifths of our Calories, half of our protein, three-quarters of our calcium, and about one-half of our vitamins (except vitamins A and D, which are not present in potatoes and bread).

There is one other point in the table to be careful about. Most

5

THE NUTRITIONAL VALUE OF FOODS, AND THEIR USE IN PLANNING MEALS

Food	Calorie value	Body-building value	Protective value	Include in the diet
Milk	Poor	Good	Good	Frequently, and at least a pint a day.
Potatoes	Poor	Poor	Fair	Once a day.
Bread	Good	Fairly good	Good	Frequently, and in quantities to satisfy appetite.
Meat and fish	Good	Good	Fairly good	Once a day.
Butter and margarine	Very good	Useless	Good	Frequently and in quantities to satisfy appetite.
Eggs	Fair	Fairly good	Fairly good	Several times a week.
Cheese	Good	Very good	Good	May replace meat or fish.
Vegetables other than potatoes	Very poor	Very poor	Good	Once a day; include a wide variety.
Fruit	Very poor	Very poor	Good	Once a day.
Sugar	Good	Useless	Useless	As desired to satisfy appetite and improve palatibility of food.
Jam, marmalade, syrup	Fairly good	Useless	Poor	

of the foods listed appear to be good sources of protective nutrients. Thus butter and margarine are listed as 'good' because they are valuable sources of vitamins A and D, but they contain no other vitamins or mineral elements. As many foods are rich in only one or two protective nutrients, it is essential that a wide variety of protective foods is included in the diet.

Some Well-balanced Meals

Using the general principles discussed above, we can plan meals that are well-balanced, varied and attractive. Here is such a set of menus for a day.

Breakfast *Fresh or tinned fruit; egg, bacon, and fried bread; toast, butter and marmalade; tea.*
 This meal has body-building foods (egg, bread and bacon), varied protective foods (fruit, butter, egg, bacon and bread) and calorie foods (mainly toast and fried bread, but also butter and marmalade). By eating plenty of toast and fried bread, large appetites may be satisfied. The tea provides water and also nutrients if it is drunk with milk and sugar; it also gives mild stimulation.

Morning snack *Milky coffee (or milk) with sugar; biscuits.*
 Most people enjoy a short break from work and a light snack during the morning, and this is quite a good habit from a nutritional point of view, especially for children and heavy manual workers. The snack suggested provides body-building nutrients (milk and biscuits), protective nutrients (milk and biscuits) and Calories (sugar, milk, biscuits).

Lunch *Meat or fish, potatoes and peas; stewed fruit and custard; water.*
 For many people lunch is the main meal of the day and it should be planned so as to be a satisfying meal. The lunch above contains body-building material (mainly meat or fish and potatoes, also milk in the custard, and peas), protective material (mainly fruit, also to a less extent the other items of the meal, except water), and Calories (mainly meat and potatoes, also peas and milk and sugar in the custard). It is good practice to include water with one meal; the body needs at least two to three pints a day, and more does no harm.

115

High tea   Cheese salad; bread, butter and jam; cakes; tea.
            This meal has body-building nutrients (mainly cheese, also bread and cakes), protective nutrients (mainly salad, also bread, butter and cakes) and energy-giving nutrients (mainly bread, butter, jam and cakes).

Bed-time   Hot milk (flavoured if desired in the form of chocolate or
snack   ovaltine); Ryvita, butter, honey.
            Before going to bed most people enjoy a light snack, and this one contains body-building nutrients (milk and Ryvita), protective nutrients (milk, Ryvita and butter) and Calories (milk, Ryvita, butter and honey).

Some Badly Planned Meals

Lunch 1   Potato soup; cornish pasties (mainly meat and potatoes in pastry), fried potatoes; steamed jam pudding; tea.
            If you had a lunch like this you should feel full of energy, but you would not be full of much else! This meal is badly balanced because it contains far too much starchy material, and very little of body-building or protective value.

Lunch 2   Chicken soup; mixed grill consisting of lamb chop, kidney and sausage, creamed potatoes; sweet omelette (made from eggs, milk, butter and jam); white coffee.
            This meal should 'build you a fine body', but it contains far too much protein at the expense of other nutrients.

Lunch 3   Tomato juice; green salad with lettuce, tomatoes, cucumber, beetroot and celery; fruit salad; tea.
            This would be a bad meal for a hard day's work; it provides few Calories and little body-building material, and contains far too much protective material.

Each of the three lunch menus just described is badly balanced because it is based mainly on foods with the same function. If you study the menus you will see that by re-arranging them you can plan three well-balanced and varied meals. Try it!

A well-balanced meal that is also varied and attractive.

Planning Attractive Meals

It is no good planning a well-balanced meal if, when it is prepared, it is so unattractive that no one will eat it! The following points should help you in planning meals that are pleasing and satisfying (see also page 126).

1. You will know the phrase 'A little of what you fancy does you good', but like most such popular sayings it is not always true. Very often it *is* a good idea to give people what they like. This is not *always* true, however, especially where people have been used to bad feeding habits. For example, children who have been brought up to eat as many sweets as they like may develop a craving for sweet foods. Thus if they are always given what they fancy they may choose sweet (Calorie) foods at the expense of body-building and protective foods.

2. A meal should *look* nice; it should be freshly prepared and served so that it looks its best. If the food is a drab colour, its appearance can be improved by adding colour, perhaps in the form of red paprika or a coloured sauce or a gravy containing 'browning'. A coloured decoration—such as a cherry, a sprig of mint or parsley, a slice of orange or tomato—may also be used to improve its appearance.

3. A meal should *smell* good. An appetizing aroma is not only pleasant in itself but it stimulates the flow of digestive juices and makes digestion easier. This is one reason for starting a meal with a good-smelling soup.

4. A meal should be *interesting*. If the same food appears twice in a meal (even if it is disguised on its second appearance!) interest is lost. Interest and variety can be obtained by including food with strong flavour alongside those with little flavour and by mixing crisp foods with soft ones.

5. Meals should take account of the *season* of the year. In hot weather cold dishes—vegetable and fruit salads, cold beverages and sweets—should be provided, while in cold weather hot sustaining foods are in demand.

6. Meals should contain some *roughage*. Porridge, bread, fruit and vegetables all contain cellulose and therefore provide roughage. Although roughage cannot be digested, it aids the muscular action of our intestines and prevents constipation.

7. All meals should provide a reasonable amount of *water*. Ideally water itself is best (it may be iced in hot weather) but it may be provided in the form of hot beverages or sauces. Sauces are particularly valuable with meals which would otherwise be rather dry. Fruit and vegetables are also useful sources of water.

8. Both *animal* and *vegetable* protein should be included in meals. For reasons already discussed (Chapter 5) animal protein foods (meat, fish, cheese) should be mixed with vegetable protein foods (potatoes, cakes and bread).

9. Meals should be eaten in *cheerful* and *relaxing* surroundings.

10. Meals should be eaten with *clean* and *attractive* utensils. Chipped or cracked crockery and stained or scratched cutlery are both unsightly and unhygienic, and should never be used. Crockery, cutlery and tablecloths should all be clean.

11. Good meals need not be *expensive*. Efficient meal planning should be economic in the sense that it provides balanced nutrients and variety at minimum cost. Expensive cuts of meat may not provide more body-building material than cheap ones. Herrings and kippers are cheaper than plaice or sole, but they have at least as high a nutritional value. The staple foods of our diet—potatoes, bread and milk—are both cheap and good nutrient providers. On the other hand many luxuries—such as frozen strawberries or asparagus and fancy cakes—are poor value for money in terms of nutrient value.

Economy in meal planning cannot be carried too far, however, because the cheapest foods are usually starchy foods. Good protein foods—meat, fish, eggs, cheese, milk—are more expensive than starchy ones, and so enough money should be spent on food to ensure that a balanced diet is obtained.

Meals for the Very Young

For the first few months of its life a baby is best breast-fed on its mother's milk. After about six months the baby should be gradually weaned and spoon-feeding started. As mother's milk is replaced by cow's milk extra vitamin C (usually from orange juice) and vitamin A and D (usually from cod liver oil) should be provided as cow's milk is not a rich source of these vitamins.

Milk is the basis of diet for the very young. Between the ages of 1–5 at least
a pint of milk should be included in the diet every day.

Sometimes babies have to be bottle-fed from birth, in which case the diluted cow's milk used must always be supplemented with orange juice and cod liver oil. Cow's milk is also lacking in iron and as soon as possible after spoon-feeding has been started, solid foods containing iron should be introduced. Sieved green vegetables, minced meats and mashed hard-boiled eggs are all suitable for this purpose.

Between the ages of one and two the baby's teeth are developing and the change from a liquid milk diet to a normal-type diet is completed. To encourage the baby to use its teeth crisp foods, such as rusks and thin toast, should be added to the diet.

After its second birthday the child's diet resembles that of an adult, except that the amounts eaten are small and meals should be rich in body-building and protective foods. At this stage milk should still be the basis of the diet, and at least a pint a day should be included (see page 120). Rich foods that are difficult to digest, such as fried foods and rich cakes, and twice-cooked foods should be avoided.

Meals for School-children

The years spent at school are the time of rapid growth and change in our bodies. It follows that meals for school-children must provide for these needs. The amounts of body-building foods needed by the body is at its greatest during this period, and the diet should therefore supply plenty of protein and calcium. Protective foods are equally important and the diet should contain plenty of foods rich in mineral elements and vitamins. In particular girls should be given plenty of iron-rich foods—meat (especially liver and kidney), green vegetables and bread—during puberty.

The early teens is a period of great physical activity and therefore of hearty appetites. School-children should eat as much energy-giving food as they feel like, and it is good practice to include plenty of fatty foods in the diet, as these are concentrated sources of Calories.

Substantial, simple and well-cooked meals are the best for school-children. Plenty of the staple foods—bread, milk and potatoes—should be provided, along with substantial amounts of meat or fish, cheese, butter or margarine, green vegetables and fresh fruit.

Meals for Adults

When we stop growing, our appetites get less because our need for food gets less. Of course we still need a balanced diet when we are fully grown, and the principles of good meal-planning already discussed should be followed.

People who are doing heavy manual work should be given more energy-rich and protein foods than people doing only light work, and so their diet should be rich in meat, cheese, sugar, milk and fat. Larger servings of potatoes and bread and butter should also be given. Hot fried meals are more desirable for such people than cold salads, because they are more sustaining and richer in Calories.

The amount of protective nutrients and body-building mineral elements needed by the body does not vary with occupation and so both heavy and light workers should be given the same amounts.

Women have smaller Calorie needs than men and so their appetites are smaller. Although women should be given less energy-rich foods than men, they should be given just as much of the protective nutrients and body-building mineral elements. In particular expectant and nursing mothers should be given plenty of body-building and protective foods.

Meals for Invalids

If you have ever been kept in bed for weeks—or even days—on end, you will know just how important meals are to an invalid. They need especial care in planning, cooking and serving.

Invalids suffering from some diseases—such as diabetes and anaemia—need special diets, and in such cases the doctor will advise what foods should be eaten. Apart from this, diets for invalids should follow certain simple rules:

1. If the invalid has a higher than normal temperature, the diet should consist of liquids only. The main items on the diet should be milk, milk beverages and jellies; nourishing soups and fruit drinks.

2. Invalids with near-normal temperatures need a light diet with only small amounts of energy-foods. Milk, eggs, fish, green vegetables and plenty of fruit should be given.

122

This delicious-looking cake would be ideal for a teenage party, but very bad for an invalid or slimming diet!

3. All the foods in the diet should be served in an easily-digestible form. Milk drinks, milk puddings and jellies; steamed fish with a tasty sauce; stewed and minced meat; lightly cooked. egg dishes; these are all suitable.
4. Foods which are difficult to digest—fried foods, tough meat, rich cakes—should not be given (see page 123).
5. As invalids are nursed back to health, the amount of protective and body-building foods in the diet should be increased. Fresh fruit is particularly valuable, and if this is not available bottled fruit juices may be used.
6. Plenty of variety should be the aim of meal planning, and as the range of desirable foods is limited, special attention should be given to the provision of tasty sauces, and a good variety of beverages and soups.
7. Food should be fresh and of good quality and served immediately after cooking. It should be served as attractively as possible.
8. Although servings should be small, meals should be frequent and regular.

Meals for Vegetarians

Strict vegetarians will eat no food that is of animal origin. This means that meat, fish, eggs, milk, cheese and butter cannot be used. Planning a balanced diet for such people is rather like planning a journey for someone who will not travel by air, road or rail!

One difficulty in planning a diet for such people is that as animal protein cannot be used, there is little prospect of including protein of high nutritional value in the diet except for foods made from soya beans. It is also difficult to provide enough mineral elements, such as calcium and iron, and fat-soluble vitamins (vitamin A and D). Even the use of soya bean foods and other nutritious foods, such as nuts and margarine, cannot prevent such a diet from being *very* bulky. It will tend to be unbalanced, with too many energy-giving foods and too few body-building and protective foods.

Fortunately not many vegetarians are strict, and most of them only exclude animal *flesh* from the diet and continue to eat such animal products as milk, eggs, butter and cheese. As all these foods contain both protective and body-building nutrients it is no longer difficult to plan a well-balanced diet. Such vegetarian

diets need not be bulky and they do not differ greatly from a 'normal' diet, except that no use is made of meat and to compensate in some measure for this, nuts and soya foods are used.

Meals for Slimming

It is fashionable nowadays to be slim, and popular magazines are full of suggestions of how to slim easily. Apart from fashion, many people are too fat, and this is undesirable as it puts a big strain on the heart and other organs.

There is one very simple rule to follow in slimming; *eat less food*! In general it is best to cut down on carbohydrate foods, but not on fatty or protein foods. Thus in planning meals for slimming the use of such foods as potatoes, bread, sugar, cakes and other sweet foods, should be limited (see page 123).

Balanced diets made up of powdered ingredients are now available for slimming purposes, but the use of these is quite unnecessary in most cases. The aim in planning a diet for slimming should be to make it as much like a normal diet as possible.

There are no short cuts to slimming, and fat people who continue with their usual diet and take 'slimming pills' in the hope of getting slim without dieting are likely to be disappointed. Such pills are likely to contain little more than a gentle laxative!

Packed Meals

Some people suppose that a packed meal always has less nutritional value than a cooked one. This is quite wrong! By careful planning and preparation a packed meal may be nutritious, well-balanced, full of variety and attractive.

Bread—in the form of sandwiches or rolls—usually forms the basis of packed meals. For the sake of variety non-sweet biscuits and crisp breads, such as Ryvita, may also be used. These are spread with butter and filled with a variety of fillings. Ham and pineapple, cheese and cucumber, egg and tomato, sardines and lettuce are all nutritious and attractive. The combination of bread, butter and filling if well planned can have nutritional value equal to that of a hot 'meat and two veg' course.

Packed meals should include either raw vegetables or fresh fruit, and milk or coffee. The beverage may be either iced or hot according to the season if a thermos flask is available. Hungry people may be satisfied by the inclusion of sweet biscuits or cake.

Tender chops that have been grilled to provide a nutritious and appetizing dish.

SUMMARY

A balanced diet is one which supplies us with all the essential nutrients in the right proportions for our needs. Such a diet cannot be based on a single food (except for breast-fed babies) and though it is possible to base it on only a few carefully chosen foods, it is wiser to use as many foods as possible.

A diet will only be balanced if it is planned with the people who will eat it in mind. A set of daily recommended allowances for each nutrient and for various types of people is available. Food tables giving the nutrient content of every food are also available. Except in certain cases, however, it is not necessary to calculate the exact nutrient content of the meals in the diet. It is enough to know which foods are rich in particular nutrients, and to make sure that every meal is balanced as far as nutrients are concerned.

In planning meals, enough foods rich in body-building and protective nutrients should be included to meet the recommended allowances and after this enough energy foods should be included to satisfy the appetite. In addition to being well balanced, meals should look, smell and taste good; they should be interesting, varied and eaten with clean utensils in cheerful and relaxing surroundings. They should contain enough water and roughage for good health and also a mixture of both animal and vegetable protein.

Meals should be planned to meet the needs of the individual concerned. The diet of young babies is based on mother's milk whereas the diets of school-children should be based on a variety of foods supplying enough body-building foods for growth, plenty of protective foods and enough energy foods for much physical activity. Meals for adults must be adapted to their occupation, while meals for invalids need special care and attention. Meals for strict vegetarians are difficult to plan because no animal foods may be included, while balanced and nutritious packed meals are easy to plan, and may have a nutrient value at least equal to that of cooked meals.

8   Cooking

Why do we eat some foods raw and others cooked? There are several reasons for this. Sometimes cooking improves the flavour of the food. For instance the flavour of uncooked flour or sour apples is not very pleasant, but when the flour has been converted into bread and the apples stewed with sugar, their flavour is much improved. On the other hand you would not cook fresh strawberries—this would spoil the delicious flavour of the raw fruit.

Cooking may also improve the attractiveness of food. You would not be very enthusiastic about eating a raw chop, but after cooking, it has an appetizing appearance and a good smell. Even more important, cooking may make a food more digestible. It would be difficult to eat the flesh of a raw chop (or uncooked flour) even if you wanted to, but after cooking, it is much more tender and so easier to chew and digest. Finally, cooking may improve the keeping quality of a food and make it safe. For example, milk may be boiled to delay the souring process and kill bacteria. The preservation of food by heat treatment is quite distinct from cooking, and is dealt with in the next chapter.

Methods of Cooking

Cooked food is food that has been changed in various ways by heat treatment. The heat may be applied in a number of ways; it may be dry or moist, it may be applied by means of fat or by infrared radiation.

1. *Dry-heat methods.* Dry heat cooking may be done in an oven. When food is cooked by heating it in an oven it is said to be *baked*. Baking is rather a slow method of cooking, but it has the advantage that large quantities of food can be cooked and the food is cooked evenly. Sometimes the food to be cooked is put into the oven in a tin containing a little fat; food cooked in this way is said to be

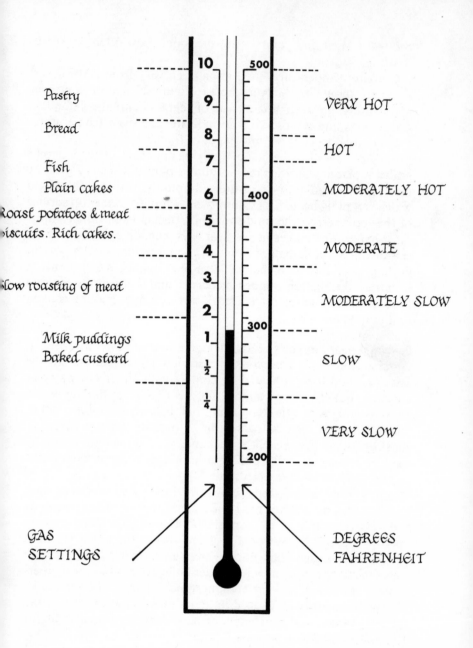

Fig. 43.   Oven temperatures.

129

roasted. Meat and potatoes are the foods most often cooked by roasting.

Cooking temperatures used in an oven vary from 200°F. (very slow) to about 500°F. (very hot). Figure 43 shows how oven temperatures are described in terms of degrees Fahrenheit, standard gas settings and words. It also indicates the oven temperatures that are used to cook various types of food.

Grilling is another method of applying dry heat. The food to be grilled is placed beneath a red-hot source of heat, usually a glowing metal grid. Radiant heat is directed onto the surface of the food which is rapidly heated. Grilling heat is applied to the top surface of the food and so the food should be turned from time to time. *Infra-red grilling* makes use of heat rays which have longer wavelengths than visible light. Some of the radiation used in normal grilling is of this kind, but in infra-red cookery the proportion of infra-red radiation is much increased, and this reduces cooking time to such an extent that a steak, for example, may be cooked in a minute.

2. *Moist heat methods.* High temperatures are used in dry heat cooking, but moist heat cooking uses low temperatures. In the latter method food is heated by contact with either hot water or steam. In *boiling*, for example, food is cooked in boiling water. In *simmering* water is kept near, but below, its boiling point. This method is also called *stewing*, especially when it refers to meat or fruit. *Poaching* is also simmering, but the term is usually used in connection with cooking fish, or eggs without their shells.

The steam produced when water boils is used in *steaming*. The steam is either used directly to heat the food, or indirectly to heat the container holding the food. Because these moist heat methods use low temperatures, they are slow. However, cooking may be speeded up by the use of a *pressure cooker*, in which steam is produced at higher than normal pressure. Increase of pressure raises the temperature at which water boils, so the cooking temperature is increased, and the cooking time reduced. For example, suet puddings may be cooked in about 50 minutes instead of the usual $2\frac{1}{2}$ hours, and tough cuts of meat may be stewed in about 15 minutes instead of at least 2 hours.

In essence a pressure cooker is a pan with a well-fitting lid arranged so that steam can be safely generated under pressure. The pan and lid lock together by means of a groove to make the

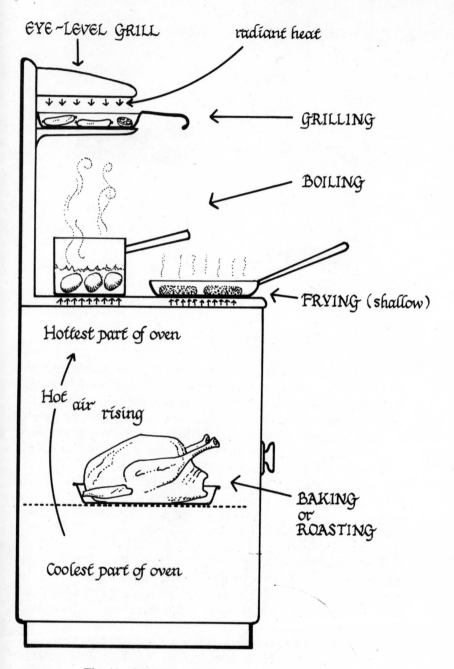

EYE-LEVEL GRILL

radiant heat

GRILLING

BOILING

FRYING (shallow)

Hottest part of oven

Hot air rising

BAKING or ROASTING

Coolest part of oven

Fig. 44.   Methods of cooking on a modern cooker.

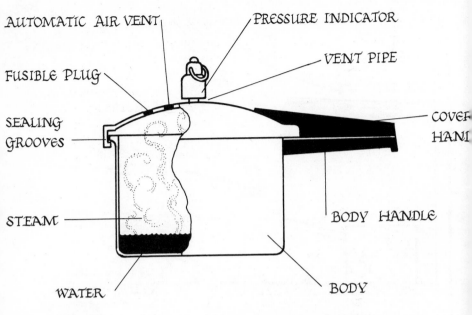

AUTOMATIC AIR VENT

PRESSURE INDICATOR

VENT PIPE

FUSIBLE PLUG

SEALING GROOVES

COVER HAND

STEAM

BODY HANDLE

WATER

BODY

Fig. 45. A pressure cooker (Presto type).

cooker pressure-tight (Fig. 45). The food to be cooked and the required amount of water are put into the pan, which is then closed. When the closed pan is heated air is driven out through the air vent until the cooker is full of steam. In pressure cookers with a pressure indicator—as shown in the diagram—the vent then closes and pressure builds up to 15 lb. per square inch. Slow heating only is then needed to maintain this pressure, which is shown by the pressure indicator. Should the pressure rise too much, steam automatically escapes through the air vent. The fusible plug is a second safety device; this melts if the cooker overheats or boils dry.

3. *Frying.* In *frying*, food is cooked in hot fat. Fat has a very much higher boiling point than water and can be heated almost to its boiling point without smoking. Frying is a quick method of cooking because of the high temperature that is used. In *shallow frying*, a shallow pan is used and enough fat is added to cover the bottom of the pan. Although such a method is quick, heating of the food is uneven and it should be turned from time to time. Lard, dripping and vegetable oils (such as olive oil, corn oil and

132

cottonseed oil often blended together as in 'Twirl' which is a mixture of the last two) are best for shallow frying. In *deep frying*, a deep pan and plenty of fat are used, so that when the food is added it is completely covered by the fat, which should be very hot. Temperatures of between 360°F. and 400°F. are usually used, and the temperature of the fat should be checked with a thermometer. Such a method is quick and the food is cooked evenly on all sides. Refined vegetable oils or cooking fats—which are made by hardening a blend of vegetable, animal and marine oil—are best for deep frying.

Effects of Cooking on Different Nutrients

Important—learn thoroughly & summarise

1. *Fats.* When fats are heated they melt and if they contain water, this is driven off as water vapour. At 212°F. fats containing water appear to boil; this is caused by the water being given off as steam. Fats are stable to heat and can be heated almost to their boiling point before they start to break down. It is because of this fact—and also because they have high boiling points—that fats are used for cooking. If they are heated too much, they break down producing an unpleasant-smelling smoke.

2. *Carbohydrates.* When starch is cooked using dry heat it darkens in colour as the starch is converted into *dextrins*, which are more easily digested than starch. Further heating causes the starch to char. These changes can be observed during the toasting of bread.

Most starchy foods are cooked using moist heat. Under these conditions the starch grains absorb moisture and swell. The grains grow to about five times their normal size and then burst. If you put a little starch in cold water and heat, you will be able to follow this process for yourself. You will notice that when the starch grains burst, *or gelatinize* as it is called, a white thickish paste is obtained. This is why starchy material—cornflour or flour perhaps—is used to thicken sauces.

Uncooked starchy foods are difficult to digest because the digestive juices are unable to penetrate the protective layer that surrounds each starch grain. Cooking not only gelatinizes the starch, but also softens and breaks down the cellulose framework of the plant. The boiling of potatoes illustrates this process. The starch grains in raw potatoes are enclosed in cellulose envelopes and as the potatoes are heated in water the cellulose softens

133

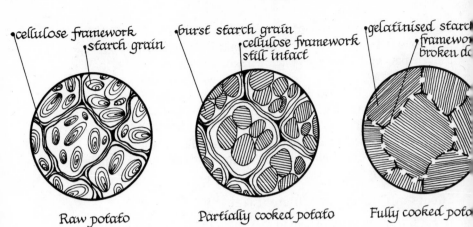

cellulose framework
starch grain

burst starch grain
cellulose framework
still intact

gelatinised starch
framewo[rk]
broken do[wn]

Raw potato   Partially cooked potato   Fully cooked pota[to]

Fig. 46.   Section of a potato before and during cooking as seen through a microscope.

and the starch grains gelatinize. When fully cooked the cellulose layers break down and the potatoes are soft and easily eaten and digested (Fig. 46).

When sugar is cooked using dry heat it melts and darkens in colour until it becomes dark brown. It is then known as *caramel*, and has a toffee-like flavour. On further heating it chars and burns.

3. Proteins. Proteins undergo great changes when they are heated. Many proteins coagulate on being heated; you will remember that egg white coagulates when it is heated above 60°C. (page 28). As proteins coagulate they become solid. For example, when milk is heated a skin forms, and this is because some of the proteins have coagulated. Cheese is another important protein food, and when this is heated it melts and on further heating some of the proteins coagulate and the cheese becomes stringy and tough.

Not all proteins coagulate on heating and this fact is important when considering how to cook protein foods. *Collagen* and *elastin*, for example, are two important insoluble proteins in meat and because they are not soluble they are not easily digested. Their presence in meat makes it tough, and as the cheaper cuts of meat usually contain more collagen and elastin than more expensive ones, they are usually tougher. Tough meat must be cooked in a way which will make it tender. If such meat is cooked with

134

dry heat the tough elastin is not changed and the collagen is hardened. So if tough cuts of meat are roasted or grilled, they do not become tender—but tougher!

Tough meat is best cooked slowly using moist heat; by stewing for example. This converts the tough collagen into *gelatin*. Gelatin is a soluble protein—it is the substance which makes jellies set or 'gel'—and so is easily digested. Elastin is not changed by moist heat, and so parts of animals which contain much elastin —such as the neck—never become tender, no matter how long they are cooked.

4. *Mineral elements.* Heat does not affect mineral salts found in food, because they are stable substances which do not break down at the temperatures used in cooking. Moist heat methods of cooking, such as stewing and boiling, cause loss of salts which are soluble in water. Boiled fish, for example, is rather tasteless because of the considerable loss of mineral salts that occurs during cooking. However, the salts are present in the water in which the fish has been boiled, and this liquid or *stock* can be used for making a tasty sauce to eat with the fish.

5. *Vitamins.* Dry heat cooking methods destroy those vitamins which are unstable to heat. Vitamin C is destroyed at quite low temperatures, and so all methods of cooking cause some loss of this vitamin. To make the loss as small as possible, foods containing vitamin C should be cooked for as short a time as possible and should be eaten as soon as they are cooked. Two of the B vitamins, thiamine and riboflavin, are unstable at high temperatures. Riboflavin is the more stable of the two, and little is lost except at high cooking temperatures, such as those used in rapid grilling. Thiamine is largely destroyed at high temperatures, such as are used in grilling and roasting.

Cooking with moist heat causes loss of water-soluble vitamins, as well as those which are destroyed at low temperatures. Vitamin C is both soluble in water and unstable to heat, and therefore some loss during cooking cannot be avoided. Vitamin C is also destroyed by oxidation in air, and this process is hastened by enzymes present in the plant or fruit. These enzymes are set free by crushing or chopping. When you cook vegetables you should take the following precautions to reduce loss of vitamin C:

(a) do not crush, and chop as little as possible

(b) put the vegetables into boiling water (thus keeping cooking time as short as possible)

(c) use as little water as possible

(d) cook gently and for as short a time as possible

(e) exclude air during cooking by having a lid on the pan

(f) eat the vegetable as soon as possible after it has been cooked.

The B vitamins are soluble in water in varying degrees, thiamine being the most soluble. A considerable proportion of the thiamine in foods may be lost during cooking, especially if they are boiled in alkaline solutions. For this reason you should not add an alkaline substance, such as sodium bicarbonate, to green vegetables to prevent loss of green colour during cooking. The amounts of the other B vitamins lost during cooking are small and not important.

Vitamin A and D are insoluble in water and stable except at high temperatures. There is therefore little, if any, loss of these vitamins during cooking.

HOW TO COOK SOME IMPORTANT FOODS

This is not a cookery book, and we have no space to give recipes for cooking any particular dishes. There are many books which do give such recipes and you will find some of these in the reading list at the end of the book. However, it is important that you understand the basic ideas of cookery, the reasons *why* we cook particular foods in one way rather than another. You will be able to do this if you understand the nature of the foods discussed in earlier chapters and the effects of cooking on the different nutrients that we have just thought about.

If you understand the reasons why we do things in cookery, you will not only find it easy to follow and understand recipes, but you will have enough knowledge to be able to take a basic recipe and adapt it in many varied and interesting ways. You will then have the thrill of being able to create your own recipes—you will be a *real* cook!

"Why won't these cook?"   A real cook!

Fig. 47.   We need to know *why* we cook a food in a particular way.

Egg Cookery

Cooking eggs is very simple; even men and boys often boast that they can boil an egg!   Egg cookery depends upon the nature of the proteins in the egg.   As we have seen, when an egg is put into hot water the proteins coagulate and the egg gradually sets.   Both dry and moist heat produce this effect, so that eggs coagulate during cooking whether they are being boiled or fried.   Eggs are digestible in all forms, but they are most easily digested when the egg white is just solid and the yolk still liquid.   If an egg is over-cooked, the white is hard and tough and the yolk breaks up into a powder.

Eggs are useful ingredients in cooking many types of dish, because of the setting effect that occurs when the egg proteins coagulate.   Eggs used in cake mixtures, for example, help to 'fix' the shape of the cake during baking.   Eggs in sauces and custards act as thickening agents.   Crumbly foods which are to be fried, such as fish cakes and rissoles, are often coated with egg before cooking.   When the egg comes into contact with the hot fat, it coagulates and forms a hard coating that seals the surface and prevents the food from falling apart, and from absorbing fat and becoming greasy.   Eggs are viscous and when added to dry ingredients, such as are used in making rissoles or croquettes, they help to bind the mixture together.   When the mixture is cooked the egg coagulates so making the binding effect permanent.

When egg white is beaten it becomes stiff because of the partial coagulation of the albumin.   If this stiff foam is gently heated

137

more coagulation occurs and it becomes rigid. This fact is the basis of making meringues. During beating, air is trapped in the egg white mixture which becomes very light. This is why egg whites are used in recipes to give lightness to the cooked product. They are used in this way, for instance, in the making of sponge cakes, in which the only ingredients are eggs, sugar and flour, plus flavouring if desired.

Rich Cakes

There are many varieties of rich cakes so we shall take one example to illustrate the main principles involved in cooking them. The traditional 'pound cake' is made from one pound of each of the four ingredients—fat, sugar, flour and eggs.

A cake recipe is chosen so that the ingredients which give volume to the final product are balanced by those that give strength to its structure. If the ingredients giving volume are present in too small a proportion, the cake does not rise properly during baking and the product is too solid. If they are present in too large a proportion, the cake mixture rises rapidly during baking but later collapses, so that the cake sinks in the middle (Fig. 48).

In the pound cake, the egg white and fat provide volume by trapping air in the mixture while the flour (which forms gluten) and eggs produce a strong structure. Sugar makes the product sweet, and also improves texture.

In order to make this rich type of cake the fat—butter for preference—is softened (but *not* melted) and then mixed with the sugar. The mixture is beaten up until it is smooth, white and

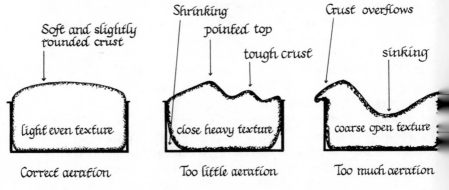

Fig. 48. Aeration of a cake mixture.

138

fluffy. This is called *creaming*, and during beating air becomes trapped in the mixture. The eggs, well beaten, may then be added, and the mixture is again beaten until it is light and foamy. The flour is gently folded in, and the mixture gently stirred until blending is complete and the mixture smooth.

The mixture is put into the oven, pre-heated to the required temperature, and cooked in a tin which has been greased and lined with greaseproof paper. During baking, the bubbles of air and water vapour trapped in the mixture expand and the cake rises. These bubbles are enclosed in an oily film containing egg white proteins, and as these proteins coagulate the film becomes rigid and the shape of the cake is 'fixed'. When baking is complete the cake structure is light, open and strong.

Raising Agents

Most cake mixtures contain a larger proportion of flour than a pound cake, and in such cases increased aeration is needed. This is supplied by a *raising agent*.

Baking soda or *sodium bicarbonate* is the simplest raising agent. When it is heated it breaks down producing carbon dioxide, which aerates the product. Unfortunately it also produces *sodium carbonate*, better known as washing soda. This substance is left behind in the mixture being baked, and, if present in large amounts, gives it an unpleasant taste. So baking soda is best used in making baked products like ginger bread and chocolate cake, which have a strong flavour of their own.

For most purposes a *baking powder* is a more suitable raising agent than baking soda. It consists of a mixture of substances which produce carbon dioxide when mixed with water and heated. Baking powders are made from baking soda, an acid substance— often either *tartaric acid* or *cream of tartar*—and some form of starch as a filler.

As long as a baking powder is kept dry it will keep well, and if it does get slightly damp, the moisture is absorbed by the filler. When it is mixed with water and heated, the baking soda reacts with the acid substance and carbon dioxide is produced.

It is important that the correct amount of baking powder is added to a mixture; too much is just as bad as too little (Fig. 49). As a matter of convenience a *self-raising flour* is sometimes used.

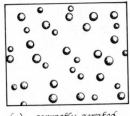
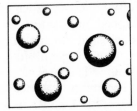

(a) correctly aerated   (b) too much aeration

Fig. 49. Cake textures, showing the small regular bubbles in a well-baked cake and the large uneven bubbles if too much baking powder is used.

As its name suggests this is flour to which a certain amount of baking powder has been added. The proportion of baking powder is such that self-raising flour is suitable for plain cakes and scones —but *not* for rich cakes. It has the disadvantage that the ratio of baking powder to flour is fixed. When you gain confidence in making cakes you will prefer to use plain flour and calculate for yourself the best amount of baking powder to use.

Plain Cakes

A rich cake is one in which the weight of fat is *more* than half the weight of flour. In a very rich cake, such as the pound cake considered earlier, the weight of fat equals the weight of flour. In very rich cakes—see table opposite—the weight of flour also equals the weight of egg. As an egg can aerate its own weight of flour, such cakes need no baking powder. As a cake mixture becomes plainer the proportion of flour to that of fat (and eggs) increases, and in general a plain cake is one in which the weight of fat is *less* than half the weight of flour. In plain cakes eggs cannot provide enough aeration, and baking powder must be used. In the plainest mixtures, such as scones, baking powder provides all the aeration, and so a greater amount is needed.

In making a plain cake the flour is sifted into a dry basin and baking powder and salt added. The fat is rubbed into the flour very thoroughly, until the mixture looks like fine breadcrumbs. The sugar and other dry ingredients, such as fruit and flavouring, are added and the whole is mixed to the right consistency with the beaten eggs and milk. The mixture should be semi-fluid so that it will not pour, but may be dropped from a spoon into a greased tin. It baked is in a moderately hot oven.

INGREDIENTS OF CAKES: COMPARATIVE WEIGHTS

Plain flour (oz.)	Fats (oz.)	Sugar (oz.)	Eggs (oz.)	Fruit (oz.)	Liquid milk (pts.)	Basic recipe	Baking powder (level tea-spoons)
8	$1\frac{1}{2}$	As required	—	Optional	$\frac{1}{4}$ approx.	Scone	4
8	3	3	2	3 to 4	$\frac{1}{4}$ approx.	Plain cake	3
8	6	6	6	6 to 8	A little	Rich cake	1
8	8	8	8	8 to 12	A little	Very rich cake	—

Choice and Purpose of Cake Ingredients

1. *Flour.*   Flour is the basis of all cakes and so it is obviously just as important to choose the right *sort* of flour as to use the right *amount.*   Flour is called *strong* if it contains a large amount of gluten (more than 10%), and *weak* or *soft* if it contains a small amount.   During baking gluten, which is a protein material, coagulates so giving strength to the mixture.   A weak flour is best for cakes as it gives a fine even texture.   Plain or household flour, which is the sort commonly used, is a blend of strong and weak flours, and though satisfactory for making cakes, does not give such a fine texture as a weak one.

2. *Sugar.*   Sugar gives cakes a sweet flavour and improves texture.   Caster sugar is the best variety, because its small crystals dissolve easily during mixing; it also creams well to give a smooth texture.

3. *Fat.*   Fat for use in cakes should have the following qualities; it should cream well so that the cake mixture is smooth and light;

141

it should make the cake 'short' by coating the starch in the flour with an oily film so that the baked cake 'melts' in the mouth; it should be neither too hard nor too soft—and it should have a good flavour. Of the various fats used in cake making, such as margarine, butter and lard, butter is the best.

4. *Eggs*. Egg white assists in trapping air and in moistening the cake mixture; it also adds strength to the structure when it coagulates on baking. Egg yolk adds richness and colour. Eggs used in cakes should be fresh and of good quality.

5. *Fruit*. Dried fruit adds sweetness and flavour to cakes. Fruit should be washed and dried before being added to the mixture (and stones should be removed if present). Also care should be taken to see that the mixture is stiff enough to support the fruit or the fruit will sink to the bottom of the cake.

Meat

Meat is cooked to make it tender, to give it a good flavour and to make it safe by killing bacteria. As we saw on page 134 dry heat cooking can only be used for tender meat. Tender cuts of meat may be roasted, grilled or fried. If a low temperature is used, soluble proteins gradually coagulate and the red colour of raw meat slowly changes to the dark brown colour of cooked meat. The proteins of the connective tissues start to shrink causing some of the 'juice' in the meat to be squeezed out. If the meat is being roasted in an open container, its surface becomes dry as moisture evaporates. This dryness can be avoided by *basting*, i.e. covering the meat with a little oil from time to time.

If a high temperature is used the cooking time is reduced. High temperature cooking rapidly *sears* the surface of the meat giving it a dark brown appearance and causing much shrinkage of connective tissue, and loss of juice. Soluble proteins tend to be more completely coagulated, and therefore harder and less digestible. Such cooking gives a rather dry and hard but well-flavoured surface to the meat.

Dry heat cooking methods do not make meat more tender because, as we have seen, the insoluble proteins collagen and elastin, which make meat tough, are not softened. Tough meat

must therefore be cooked using moist heat; for example, by stewing or boiling. Such cooking converts collagen into soluble gelatin.

Cooking with moist heat is slow, soluble proteins being coagulated only slowly and collagen being slowly converted into gelatin. Soluble nutrients, mainly mineral salts and thiamine, and *meat extractives*—which are the flavouring agents that give meat its special flavour—pass into the cooking water. Boiled or stewed meat is therefore less tasty than roasted meat. This is not usually important, however, because the liquor in which the meat is cooked is usually eaten with the meat. In making a stew or hot pot, the meat is cut into small pieces and the cooking liquor is used for cooking vegetables, herbs and spices which are eaten with the meat.

Because normal moist heat cooking of meat is slow, a pressure cooker may conveniently be used to make it quicker. For example, an Irish stew which takes two hours to cook by simmering, only takes about a quarter of an hour in a pressure cooker.

Fish

The changes which occur when fish is cooked are similar to those which take place when meat is cooked. As fish contains less connective tissue than meat and no elastin it is much less tough, and cooking is not needed to make it tender, but only to make it more palatable.

Fish may be cooked using dry or moist heat. If dry heat is used soluble proteins are coagulated and some shrinkage occurs. Fish shrinks less than meat because of the smaller amount of connective tissue that it contains. As fish shrinks water evaporates from its surface leaving behind a deposit of flavouring matter and mineral salts. This makes the surface of the cooked fish very tasty.

If fish is cooked using moist heat, for instance by steaming or poaching, loss of soluble matter is greater than in dry heat methods. As fish contains less mineral salts and extractives than meat, such fish tends to be rather tasteless. It is usually eaten with a tasty sauce, which may be made from the liquor in which the fish was cooked.

Potatoes are cooked to break down the cellulose framework of the starch grains. This occurs in both dry and moist

Vegetables

Green vegetables should be cooked until their cellulose has been softened enough to make them *just* tender. Cooking should be carried out in such a way that as much vitamin C as possible is preserved (see page 135).

In cooking **starchy vegetables,** such as potatoes, not only must the cellulose framework of the plant be broken down, but starch must be gelatinized to make it digestible (see page 133). As potatoes are about four-fifths water, starch grains are gelatinized by both dry and moist heating methods. Potatoes may therefore be cooked by any method, with the result that they can be served in a large variety of ways (see page 144).

If potatoes are boiled, mineral salts and vitamin C are lost to the cooking water. Additional amounts of vitamin C are destroyed by heat, so that peeled potatoes loose about half their vitamin C during boiling. To keep these losses as small as possible potatoes should be put into boiling water so that the water *just* covers them and cooked until they are *just* tender, Cooking time may be reduced to 8–10 minutes by using a pressure cooker, and the loss of vitamin C is less. Pressure cookers are particularly useful for cooking vegetables, such as beetroot and artichokes, which take a long time to cook by boiling.

Frozen vegetables are now readily available and most of them are put into the cooking water while still frozen. Otherwise they are cooked in the same way as fresh vegetables, using the minimum amount of water. The time taken for cooking is about half that needed for the fresh variety.

SUMMARY CHARTS

Effect of cooking on nutrients

Nutrient	Effect of moist heat	Effect of dry heat
Fats	Melt to oil	Melt to oil. At very high temperatures smoke, then burn.
Carbohydrates Starch	Starch grains absorb moisture, swell and burst	Converted to dextrins, char.
Cellulose	Softens until cellulose framework of plants breaks down	—
Sugar	Forms syrup, turns to caramel, chars	Converted to caramel, chars.
Proteins	Many proteins slowly coagulate, e.g. egg white. Insoluble proteins may be converted to soluble ones, e.g. collagen converted to gelatin, or unchanged, e.g. elastin	Many coagulate, e.g. albumin of egg white. Insoluble proteins may be hardened, e.g. collagen, or unchanged, e.g. elastin.
Mineral salts	Soluble salts are partly lost to the cooking water	Most are stable to heat, a few break down, e.g. baking soda.
Vitamins Vitamin A	Insoluble in water, not affected	Not affected.
Thiamine	Soluble in water, some lost	Destroyed at high temperatures.
Riboflavin	Slightly soluble in water, very little lost	Destroyed at very high temperatures.
Vitamin C	Soluble in water, destroyed	Destroyed at low temperatures.
Vitamin D	Insoluble in water, not affected	Not affected.

Methods of cooking

Way in which heat is applied	Method of cooking	Definition	Examples
Dry heat	Baking	Cooking carried out in an oven	Potatoes, fish, cakes.
	Roasting	Baking with the addition of fat	Large joints of tender meat, potatoes.
	Grilling	Using direct radiant heat	Small cuts of tender meat, e.g. chops and steak; fish.
Moist heat	Boiling	Using boiling water	Eggs, large joints of tough meat, vegetables, fish.
	Stewing and poaching	Using hot water below its boiling point	Meat in stews and hot pots. Fruit, fish, eggs.
	Steaming	Using steam from boiling water	Fish, vegetables, suet puddings.
	Pressure cooking	Using water boiling above its normal boiling point	Meat, vegetables such as beetroot which cook slowly in boiling water. In general used for foods which take a long time to cook by normal boiling or steaming.
Fat	Frying	Using hot fat	Meat, often as rissoles or sausages. Potatoes, eggs, fish.
Infra-red cooking	Equivalent to rapid grilling	Using infra-red radiation	Small tender cuts of meat.

9 The Preservation of Food

When food is kept for any length of time it may go 'bad' and become unfit to eat. This is common knowledge and we all know that some foods are more perishable than others. Milk and bread, for example, can be kept for only a few days whereas other foods such as flour, jam and sugar stay unchanged for much longer periods. Butter, bacon, cheese, salted meat, dried fruit and several similar foods were first made centuries ago in an attempt to convert surplus perishable foods into more permanent forms.

Up to about one hundred and fifty years ago most people in Europe lived in villages or small towns, and most occupations were connected directly in some way or other with the land. Tastes in food varied from on the one hand the gigantic meals consumed by the comfortably off (you can today sometimes see the menus framed in hotels), to the rather monotonous diet of the poor. Their food consisted largely of bread, butter, cheese, peas, turnips and other garden produce. Potatoes were introduced in the eighteenth century. Meat was expensive, though many were able to supplement their meat diet by poaching. None the less those who could afford (legally) to eat meat once a week were fortunate. Before the introduction of turnips as a winter food for cattle in the early part of the eighteenth century, farm animals were killed in mid-winter when the stocks of hay were exhausted. Great feasts were held to mark the occasion when as much as possible of the fresh meat was eaten. The remainder was salted so that it would keep after a fashion for the rest of the winter. The only fresh meat available during this period was the flesh of wild animals. By the end of the winter the salted meat was unwholesome and was made more attractive by the liberal use of herbs and spices.

Up to about 1850 the nation's diet was rather restricted, not only because of the limited number of locally grown foods, but

also because of transport difficulties. The transport of food from one side of the world to the other or, indeed, from one part of the country to another, was so slow and difficult, that people had to be content with food which was grown in their own neighbourhood and often on their own land. In any case large scale movement of perishable foods was impossible until the coming of the railways.

To-day our diet is much more varied and interesting. This is in part due to the speed-up of transport, but it is also due to the development of methods of preserving food. We shall now consider why food goes bad, and then discuss ways in which it may be preserved.

Why Food Goes Bad

The most important cause of food spoilage is attack by small creatures known as micro-organisms which eat the food and make it unattractive to humans. Individual micro-organisms are invisible to the naked eye and are smaller than the smallest speck of dust. The micro-organisms may be *moulds, yeasts* or *bacteria*.

We have all seen moulds growing on food that is old. For example, bread will quickly become mouldy if kept for more than a few days. Strange as it may seem, the fact that mould growth has occurred does not necessarily mean that the food is unfit to eat. However, the presence of mould growth is usually a good indication that the food is old or has been stored in poor conditions. Moulds will grow on all types of food but they are particularly fond of meat, cheese and sweet foods. They grow best in a moist atmosphere at a temperature of 20–40°C. At lower temperatures moulds grow more slowly but growth can occur even at the temperature of a normal household refrigerator. Moulds grow from tiny cells called spores which are carried in the atmosphere. When mould spores settle on food they infect it and if the mould grows the food will, of course, become mouldy. Moulds and their spores are rapidly destroyed at the temperature of boiling water.

Yeasts are similar in many respects to moulds but they grow only on sugary foods. They consume the sugar and convert it to alcohol and in this way obtain the energy they need to grow and multiply. They grow best in roughly the same temperature range

as moulds, and, like moulds, they grow more slowly at lower temperatures and can be destroyed by boiling water.

The third type of micro-organism which causes food spoilage is the bacterium. Bacteria multiply very rapidly in warm moist conditions and thousands of millions of bacteria can arise from one individual in the space of a few days. They can be destroyed by heating but are more difficult to kill than moulds and yeasts. Some types are more resistant to heat than others, and the nature of the food in which they are found also influences the ease with which bacteria can be killed by heating. In acidic foods, such as fruits, bacteria die rapidly at the temperature of boiling water but in non-acid foods, such as vegetables and meat, they can withstand much higher temperatures.

Micro-organisms are present in water, dust, soil, sewage and on the hands of workers. As a result their presence in food is more-or-less inevitable. They are not all harmful, however, and some of the most prized food flavours in cheeses and fermented foods are the result of the growth of micro-organisms. On the other hand, some *are* harmful and their presence in food may cause *food poisoning* (see Chapter 10). If food is to be kept in its original condition for any length of time it is essential that the growth of micro-organisms is prevented as far as possible. This can be done either by killing the micro-organisms and preventing further attack, or by storing the food in conditions which are unfavourable for their growth.

Preservatives

The micro-organisms in a food can be killed by treatment with a chemical which poisons them. If sufficient of the chemical is left in the food it will act as a preservative and prevent further attack by micro-organisms. This is the basis of preservation by smoking, which has been used for preserving fish and meat for many centuries. The food is hung in the smoke from burning wood, and chemicals in the wood-smoke kill any micro-organisms on the food and help to prevent further attack.

Many chemicals are known which will poison micro-organisms, but unfortunately most of them are poisonous to human beings as well and so are unsuitable for use in foods. Substances which are harmful to man may not be used as preservatives. This has not

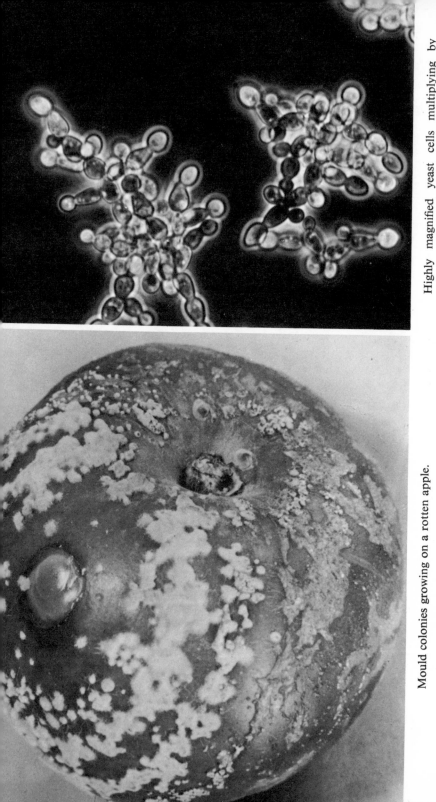

Highly magnified yeast cells multiplying by budding.

Mould colonies growing on a rotten apple.

always been the case, however, and at one time it was common for milk suppliers to add a chemical called *formalin* to milk to keep it fresh. When we realize that formalin is extremely poisonous, the folly of this practice becomes obvious.

At the present time only a handful of chemicals, known as *permitted preservatives*, may be added to food to preserve it. One of these is the choking gas sulphur dioxide which is used in sausages and soft drinks among other foods. The maximum amount that can be used varies from food to food, but in no case does it exceed three parts per thousand parts of the food. Some people can taste extremely small amounts of sulphur dioxide, but when foods containing it are cooked most of it is driven off. Even the permitted preservatives may only be used in certain foods. These are mainly bottled goods such as pickles, sauces, fruit juices and soft drinks. Such foods are not eaten at one sitting but may be in use over a period of time and the preservative prevents attack by micro-organisms during this period.

Dehydration

Micro-organisms, like all other living things, cannot grow and reproduce without water. If the water content of a food is reduced to below a certain level micro-organisms will not flourish on it. Food has been preserved by drying, or *dehydration* as it is called, for many centuries and dried fish and meat have been known for about four thousand years. Dried vegetables have been used for about a hundred years, mainly by armies and sailors who are unable to buy fresh produce. Dried soups have been known for much longer and a cake of dried soup taken by Captain Cook on his voyage round the world in 1772 still exists. This dried soup, which at that time was known as 'portable soup', looks (and probably tastes!) much like a cake of glue.

Not all the water need be removed from a food to make it unattractive to micro-organisms. Jam, for example, contains about 25% water but it can be kept for long periods without harm. This is because it also contains about 70% of sugar which dissolves in the water and makes it unavailable to micro-organisms. In fact, when micro-organisms are placed in contact with such concentrated solutions, water is absorbed from them and they die. If jam is made incorrectly so that it contains too little sugar it may easily go mouldy.

Condensation of water on the surface of jam may also reduce the sugar concentration at this point to such an extent that spots of mould may appear. The bulk of the jam is unaffected, however, and may be safely eaten after the mould has been skimmed off. Condensed sweetened milk stays wholesome for a considerable period after the tin is opened for the same reason; namely that the concentration of sugar is so high. The preservation of meat and vegetables by salting also depends on the fact that the salt dissolves in the water to form a more concentrated solution than can be tolerated by micro-organisms.

Water can be removed from food by drying it in the sun and this method is still used in some countries for drying fish and fruit such as grapes and plums. Modern methods of dehydration, however, are much more complicated than this. The food is usually chopped up and spread out in thin layers over which a current of hot air is passed. A disadvantage of this method is that the food is partially cooked in the process. In another method, called *vacuum drying*, the food is heated in a specially designed oven while the pressure in the oven is reduced by pumps, which suck out some of the air. The temperature needed to remove the water by this method is less than that required in the other method of drying, and so the food remains uncooked.

In the most up-to-date method the food is first frozen and then the water is removed by pumping away all the air from around the food with powerful pumps. This method is called *freeze drying*, and it has the advantage that the food need not be cut up beforehand. You may think it strange that food can be dried while it is frozen, but even frozen washing on a clothes line will dry if it is given enough time. Freeze drying is expensive but the product is far superior to that obtained by other methods of drying. After adding water to freeze-dried food it is almost the same as fresh food.

The great advantage of dehydrated food is its lightness and compactness compared with fresh food. This is especially true for foods like potatoes which contain large amounts of water. The powder obtained by dehydrating one ton of potatoes occupies only eight cubic feet and so it can be packed into a box only two foot square! This means that dehydrated foods are easily transported and so are especially valuable for emergency use in feeding large numbers of people.

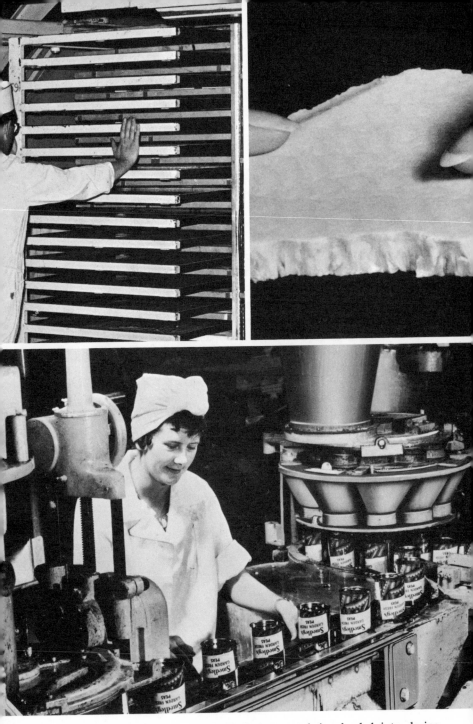

Top: Freeze drying eggs—(Left) Frozen egg being loaded into drying cabinet. (Right) Freeze dried egg is light and brittle. *Bottom: Canning peas*—Hot peas and boiling brine are filled into cans (right) which are sealed (left) before sterilizing.

Canning

Micro-organisms in food can be killed by heating. If the food is heated in a closed container, such as a glass jar or metal can, micro-organisms are unable to get at it to re-infect it. This is the basis of preservation by bottling and canning. The method was discovered by the Frenchman Nicholas Appert in the closing years of the eighteenth century and it has been an important method of food preservation ever since. In 1795 the government of France had offered a prize of 12,000 francs to anyone who could discover a method for keeping food fresh for long periods. France was at that time involved in the Napoleonic wars and was having difficulty in supplying her forces with food. Appert's products were tested by the French navy in 1806 and were so highly thought of that he received the prize. Appert used glass bottles and these are still used quite a lot in the home. It was not long, however, before cans were used instead of bottles. They were all made by hand and energetic use of a hammer and chisel was needed to open them.

For many years after their discovery, canned foods were expensive because of the cost of the cans. A first-class tinsmith could make about ten cans a day compared with the four hundred cans a minute which modern machines are capable of turning out. Nevertheless canned food became popular—especially with sailors. Before the development of canned foods the only way of obtaining meat, other than rather unpleasant salted meat, on board ship was to carry the animals and slaughter them at sea. Tinned meat was obviously much more satisfactory.

Nowadays millions of tons of food of all sorts are canned every year. The cans—an abbreviation of the word canister—are made from sheet steel coated with a very thin layer of tin. The tin coating is only about 0·00005 inch thick and its purpose is to prevent the steel from corroding. Although the containers are often called 'tins' it should be remembered that their tin content is very small. For some foods the inside surface of the can is lacquered with a special varnish which prevents blackening of the tin coating.

Food intended for canning is carefully cleaned and, where necessary, peeled. Fruit and vegetables may be 'blanched' by boiling water or steam to soften them and to make it easier to pack them into the can. The prepared food is placed in cans which are then filled with hot liquid to within about a quarter of an inch of the

top.   Sugar syrup is used for fruits and salt water for vegetables. The cans are heated almost to the boiling point of water to expel air and the lid is then sealed on.   The can is now ready for heat-sterilization or 'processing' as it is called.   The temperature to which it is heated depends upon the kind of food in the can, and the time for which it is heated upon the size of the can.   Acid foods need only be heated to the boiling point of water (212°F.) but non-acid foods are processed at 240–260°F.   The heating period lasts for 10–30 minutes for fruits and 25–50 minutes for vegetables. Large cans are heated for a longer period than small ones because of the extra time needed for the heat to penetrate to the middle of the food.

Canned foods will keep for long periods if the cans are not rusted.   In 1958 some very old cans of food were opened and the contents examined.   The plum pudding in a tin sealed in 1900 was found to be in excellent condition.   Meat canned in 1823 was found to be free from attack by micro-organisms, but the fat had partly broken down into glycerol and fatty acids.   A number of fifty-year-old cans which had been taken on Antarctic expeditions by Scott and Shackleton and brought back unopened, were also found to be perfectly wholesome.

Although we do not normally regard pasteurization of milk as a method of preservation, it certainly improves its keeping qualities. Pasteurization is intended to kill the *tubercle bacillus* and other harmful bacteria which may be present in milk from infected cows.   The drinking of infected milk can cause tuberculosis in human beings.   Milk is pasteurized by heating to at least 161°F. for at least 15 seconds and then rapidly cooling it.   Sterilized milk is given a much more severe heat treatment and, although it is sold in bottles, it is really a form of canned milk.   The milk is first *homogenized* by heating to 145°F. and forcing it through a small hole.   This breaks up the oil droplets into very small particles, and reduces the tendency of the fat in the milk to form a separate cream layer during storage.   The milk is then placed in bottles which are sealed with metal caps before heating at 220–230°F. for 30–40 minutes.   Sterilized milk will keep for at least a week and usually much longer.

Canned foods are quite as good, from a nutritional point of view, as the corresponding fresh foods.   In fact they may be better because they are often canned within a few hours of being picked.

Refrigeration

Micro-organisms do not multiply nearly as rapidly at low temperatures as at normal temperatures. This is taken advantage of in the ordinary domestic refrigerator, which is used for keeping food for short periods. The temperature in such a refrigerator is usually about 5°C., which is sufficient to chill food and reduce the activity of micro-organisms. It should be emphasized, however, that foods will only keep for short periods at this temperature.

The use of low temperatures to preserve food is by no means new. The famous author and philosopher, Francis Bacon, is reputed to have died in 1626 as a result of a chill caught while gathering snow to stuff a chicken in an attempt to preserve it! During the eighteenth century large underground chambers called ice-houses became common in large country houses. Ice and snow collected during the winter months was kept for as long as it would last in these primitive refrigerators. This was the only way in which ice could be obtained out of season in any quantity before the development of artificial refrigeration.

Beef cooled by ice was first carried from America to Europe in the 1870's. Unfortunately at the end of the voyage, which took over three months, much of the meat was found to be unfit to eat. Since then many thousands of tons of chilled meat have been successfully transported from South America in refrigerated holds. The meat is chilled to about −1°C. and at this temperature will remain in good condition for about a month.

The water present in chilled food is not frozen despite the temperature of −1°C., because dissolved solids present in the water lower its freezing point. At temperatures below −10°C., however, the water present in most foods is frozen and the growth of micro-organisms is impossible. In addition many—but not all—bacteria are killed and such foods can be safely kept for very long periods. Use is made of this fact in transporting meat from Australia and New Zealand to this country. The meat is kept at −10°C. or below both on the ship and after arrival in this country.

All types of frozen food are now available commercially. The freezing must be carried out *quickly* because slow freezing produces large ice crystals (Fig. 50). The expansion which occurs when water freezes may rupture the tissues of the food if large ice crystals are formed. This spoils the texture of the food and may

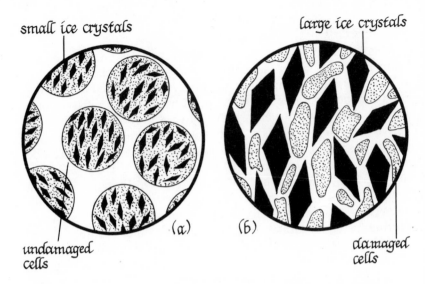

small ice crystals   large ice crystals

(a)   (b)

undamaged cells   damaged cells

Fig. 50. Formation of ice crystals in food: (a) the small crystals which result from quick freezing and (b) the large crystals resulting from slow freezing.

cause it to 'weep' on thawing. In frozen-food factories temperatures of -35 to $-40°C$. are used to cool the food as quickly as possible to the storage temperature of $-18°C$.

Quick-frozen (or deep-frozen as it is sometimes called) fruits, fish, vegetables, poultry and many types of cooked food, such as cakes, pies and chipped potatoes, are being preserved by this method in increasing quantities. In addition to buying quick-frozen food in shops, deep-freeze cabinets can be bought for freezing food at home. When thawed, frozen food should be equivalent in all respects to fresh food, provided that care was taken to see that the fresh food was clean and in perfect condition before it was frozen.

Conclusion

In general it is better to preserve food by non-chemical methods —such as canning, dehydration or refrigeration—than to use chemicals. Chemical methods of preservation are open to abuse since by using a sufficient quantity of chemicals unhygienic practices in the preparation and handling of food can be disguised. A good method of food preservation must be cheap and efficient,

Quick-freezing of peas which are seen moving through a freezer tunnel.

and the preserved food should closely resemble fresh food when it is eaten. Refrigeration is probably the best method at the moment but when the freeze-drying process has been developed sufficiently it will be as important a method of preservation as quick-freezing is to-day.

SUMMARY

When foods are kept they may be attacked by micro-organisms and become unfit to eat. The micro-organisms involved are very small living creatures known as moulds, yeasts and bacteria. They can all be killed by heating, and grow more slowly at low temperatures.

The main methods of food preservation are:

1. *Addition of preservatives. Chemical preservatives kill micro-organisms and so prevent their growth on food.*

2. *Dehydration. Micro-organisms require water to grow and reproduce. If the water content of a food is reduced to below a certain level it is no longer attractive to micro-organisms.*

3. *Canning and bottling. The micro-organisms are killed by heating and cannot re-infect the food because it is in a sealed container.*

4. *Refrigeration. This cuts down the rate of growth of micro-organisms and if the temperature is low enough (as in deep-freezing) can prevent it altogether.*

Salmonella when in contact with food destroys it at Staphyloccus when in contact will food will not destroy it at once until they turn poisonous then it will.

10   Food and Hygiene

It is useless to plan a carefully balanced diet and produce well cooked meals, if when we eat we suffer from stomach pains or other ill-effects.   We must always take the greatest possible care to see that the food we eat is as clean and safe as it can be.

Food Poisoning

If we eat food that has gone bad or been infected in some way we may suffer from *food poisoning*.   We saw in the last chapter (page 149) that the air we breathe, the things we touch and the food we eat all contain minute organisms called *bacteria*.   We noted that although many types of bacteria are harmless, there are some that are definitely harmful.   It is these disease-producing or *pathogenic* bacteria that cause food poisoning.

We cannot prevent *some* harmful bacteria entering our bodies, but we must ensure that their numbers are kept small.   If this is so, they will have little or no effect on us.   It is only when our systems are invaded by large numbers of pathogenic bacteria that we suffer from food poisoning.   Bacteria multiply so rapidly in favourable conditions (for example warmth and moisture) that thousands of millions of bacteria may arise from a single bacterium in only a few days.   It is obvious therefore that food must be stored and prepared in conditions that are unfavourable to bacterial growth.

Most food poisoning in Britain is caused by the *Salmonella* group of bacteria.   These poisonous bacteria cause diarrhoea, stomach pains, sickness and, in severe cases, death.   They are mainly spread by infected people who handle food—especially if they touch food with unwashed hands after using the toilet (see page 161).   The droppings of infected mice and rats, food—such as milk, meat and manufactured meat products—from infected animals, also lead to food poisoning from *Salmonella* bacteria.

160

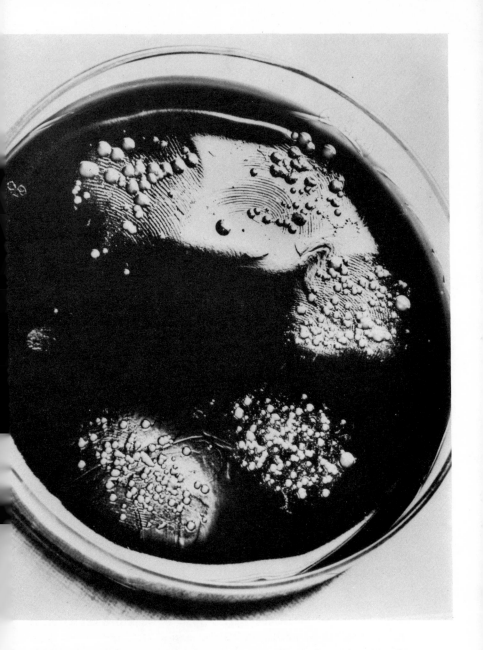

A set of fingerprints obtained from an unwashed hand after using the toilet.
The invisible bacteria on the hand have been allowed to grow on a nutrient
jelly until they have developed into visible colonies.

Food poisoning may also be caused by bacteria which produce their poison in the food. The *Staphylococcus* group of bacteria act in this way. The effects of such poisoning are rather like bad sea-sickness and include sickness and extreme weakness. These bacteria are mainly spread from the nose and mouth (by coughs and sneezes) and from cuts and scratches on the hands of infected people who handle food.

Infection from *Staphylococcal* bacteria will only cause food poisoning if the poison is given time to form. This can be prevented by cooking food thoroughly immediately after preparation. It should also be cooled rapidly after it has been cooked. If infected food is allowed to stand in warm moist conditions for any length of time, the bacteria multiply and poison is formed. The poison is rather resistant to heat treatment and subsequent cooking may fail to destroy it once it is formed.

Food which is cooked and then stored for some time in warm moist conditions may cause food poisoning even though cooking has destroyed all the bacteria. This is explained by the fact that when some bacteria find themselves in conditions which do not favour growth, they develop *spores* which are resistant to heat. The spores therefore survive cooking and if such food is stored in warm moist conditions the spores go back to their active form and multiply rapidly. Thus if such food—especially cooked meat products—is badly stored it can easily cause food poisoning.

Personal Hygiene

Pathogenic bacteria are found both inside the body and on its surface, and such bacteria may be transferred to food by people who handle it if precautions are not taken. Infection may be spread in this way both in factories during food manufacture, and during preparation and cooking of food in restaurants, canteens and homes. It cannot be urged too strongly that personal hygiene is of the greatest importance at *all* times, and *especially* when handling food.

Bacteria from the bowels find their way onto the hands during use of the toilet (see page 161), and it is therefore essential to wash the hands properly afterwards. Food handlers should keep their finger nails short and clean, and wash their hands before touching food. Everyone should wash their hands before eating a meal.

Fig. 51. Simple rules of personal hygiene.

It is true that 'coughs and sneezes spread diseases' and when coughing or sneezing the mouth and nose should be covered with a clean handkerchief.

Cuts, scratches, pimples, boils, etc., collect bacteria and should always be covered with a waterproof dressing. It is also good practice for food handlers to wear clean protective clothing to cover both the body and the hair. Such clothing should be washed frequently.

It is most important that these simple rules of personal hygiene should be carried out. As you look at Fig. 51 ask yourself if *you* always carry them out as a matter of normal routine.

HYGIENE IN THE KITCHEN

Personal hygiene is most important, but by itself it is not enough. *Every* aspect of food storage, handling and preparation must be carried out in a hygienic way. It only needs *one* weak link in a chain to make the chain snap. In a similar way it only needs *one* stage of food preparation to be unhygienic for the chance of infection to occur (Fig. 52).

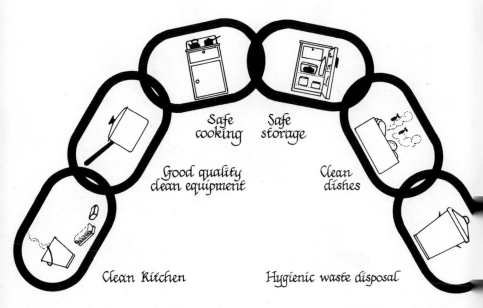

Safe
cooking

Safe
storage

Good quality
clean equipment

Clean
dishes

Clean Kitchen

Hygienic waste disposal

Fig. 52. Aspects of kitchen hygiene—essential links in the chain.

164

The Kitchen

There is more activity in the kitchen than in any other part of the house, and as the housewife does the greater part of her work there, it is important that the kitchen should be pleasant, efficient and clean. Otherwise—if, for example, the lighting is bad, the floor uneven or the sink the wrong height—the work done there will suffer. In order to keep the kitchen clean, all wall, floor and working surfaces should be smooth without any cracks or other places where dirt or insects can lodge.

Modern science makes it possible to build really attractive and efficient kitchens that should be a pleasure to work in. Walls covered with gleaming porcelain tiles, gaily coloured working surfaces of hard plastic (e.g. Formica) and smooth linoleum or thermoplastic flooring are all attractive, practical and easily kept clean.

Working surfaces should be washed down after using them for the preparation of food. Floors should be kept covered with a film of non-slip polish as this will prevent grease and dirt from becoming engrained in the surface. The polished surface is easily kept clean and shining with an occasional wipe over. Walls, ceiling and lights should be cleaned thoroughly as they have to withstand both grease and steam, and also fumes from the cooker.

When washing these kitchen surfaces a hot detergent solution should be used, and it is a good plan to add a little disinfectant to the water, so that bacteria are killed.

Kitchen Equipment

All equipment used in the kitchen must be kept spotlessly clean. It is important that such equipment should be made of suitable material and of good quality. For example, the cooking stove and its equipment are important items in frequent use. The stove will usually be heated by gas or electricity. It should have a hard-wearing easily cleaned finish, such as vitreous enamel, and the main parts should be easily detachable for cleaning. Figure 53 shows some good design features of a modern cooker that make it both safe and easy to clean.

The nature of the pans used on a stove are important. They are usually round in shape for ease of stirring and cleaning. They should be made of good quality metal and should be of even thickness to help prevent burning the food cooked in them. The

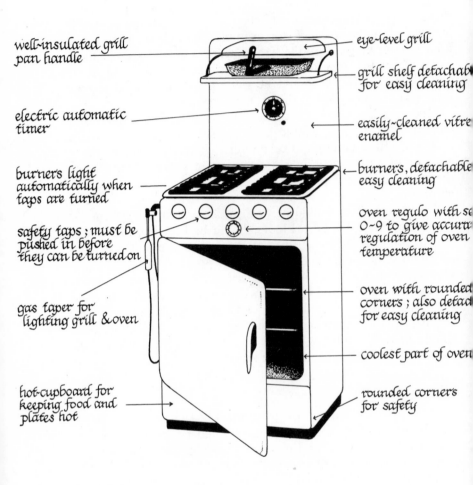

well-insulated grill pan handle

eye-level grill

grill shelf detachable for easy cleaning

electric automatic timer

easily-cleaned vitre enamel

burners light automatically when taps are turned

burners, detachable easy cleaning

safety taps; must be pushed in before they can be turned on

oven regulo with se 0~9 to give accura regulation of oven temperature

gas taper for lighting grill & oven

oven with rounded corners; also detach for easy cleaning

coolest part of oven

hot-cupboard for keeping food and plates hot

rounded corners for safety

Fig. 53.   Good design features of a modern gas cooker.

166

metal used should be reasonably hard and scratch resistant, a good conductor of heat, resistant to attack by acids and alkalis and non-poisonous. Such pans should have well-fitting lids and the handles should be well insulated and easy to grip.

Pans should always be cleaned properly after use. Cleaning may be made easier if the pan is first soaked in water before washing, hot water being used for greasy remains and cold water for starchy or protein remains. A hot detergent solution is a suitable cleaning agent, with the aid of a stiff nylon or wire brush if necessary. Care should always be taken to avoid scratching the pan, and harsh abrasives should not be used. Soda may be used to help clean greasy pans, except aluminium pans which are attacked by soda and other alkalis.

After they have been washed, pans should be carefully dried and stored upside down so that air can get in, but dirt cannot.

Metal pans with an inside surface of *silicone* are now available. They have the advantage that food does not stick to them so making them easy to clean.

The Storage of Food

If food is stored in warm moist conditions, bacterial growth will be encouraged and the food will soon become tainted. Food should therefore be stored in a cool dry atmosphere. Larders should be designed so that these necessary cool dry conditions are easily maintained. Plenty of ventilation should be provided; windows should face north and be fitted with fly-proof gauze. All parts of the larder should be cleaned frequently and strong-smelling foods should be kept in covered containers, so that the flavour of other stored foods is not spoilt.

In winter even perishable foods, such as milk and meat, can safely be kept for a day in a larder. In summer, however, such foods deteriorate rapidly and are best kept in a refrigerator. The temperature of a domestic refrigerator is about 5°C. and this is low enough to store perishable foods for several days. Such a temperature reduces the activity of bacteria, but does not kill them and so perishable foods will start to deteriorate if kept at this temperature for more than a few days.

The way different foods should be stored in a refrigerator is shown in Fig. 54. Foods that need to be stored at the lowest temperature, such as raw meat and fish, should be placed

immediately under the cooling unit. Other foods, such as vegetables and fruit, are best stored at slightly higher temperatures and should be stored at the bottom of the refrigerator. Food kept in a refrigerator should be stored in covered containers, to prevent both drying and contamination by strong-smelling foods. Covered glass or plastic containers and polythene bags are suitable for this purpose.

If perishable foods are to be stored for a long period, temperatures below 5°C. must be used. Domestic deep-freeze cabinets operate at $-20°C.$ to $-30°C.$, and at these temperatures most perishable foods can be kept for up to a year. Such foods are of course frozen solid, and when they are removed from the deep-freeze they should be allowed to 'thaw out' before being eaten. Quick-frozen foods bought from shops may also be stored for long periods in such cabinets (Fig. 54) provided that they have not been allowed to thaw out.

Safe Cooking

It is best to cook perishable food when it is as fresh as possible, though often some storage cannot be avoided. Once out of storage, food should be cooked at once.

Food should be cooked thoroughly so that it is cooked all through and not just at the surface. This applies especially to manufactured meat dishes, such as sausages, meat pies and rissoles. For such foods, which are liable to infection if not manufactured and stored under hygienic conditions, cooking must be sufficient to kill most bacteria.

After cooking, food which is not to be eaten hot, should be cooled rapidly and not allowed to stand in a warm kitchen. Warmth and moisture encourage bacterial growth, and although active bacteria may have been killed during cooking, heat resistant spores may become active and start multiplying. Food may also become reinfected with more bacteria.

If food cannot be eaten immediately after it has been cooked it should be stored in a cool larder or refrigerator. Foods such as gravy, soup and stock are ideal for bacterial growth and should not be stored.

If food is to be re-cooked after storage special care is necessary. This is because poison which is resistant to heat may develop during storage. In summer months cooked meat dishes, such as

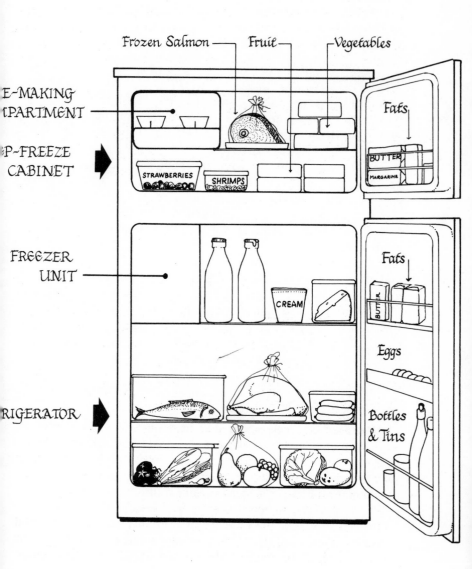

Fig. 54.   Storage of food in a refrigerator and deep-freeze unit.

stews, pies and mince, are particularly liable to infection in this way. If such dishes are re-cooked, they should never be merely warmed through as this will fail to destroy the poison. They must be heated to a high temperature, and cooking must be continued until heat has penetrated right through the food.

The Kitchen Sink

Although badly washed dishes may *look* clean, they may in fact be covered by a thin film of grease containing bacteria. It is important that dish-washing is carried out properly so that dishes not only look clean but *are* clean.

Before washing up, food remains should be scraped off plates and dishes. The dishes should then be put into a sink containing a hot detergent solution. It is also good practice to add a little disinfectant to the washing up water. After dishes, utensils and cutlery have been thoroughly washed, they should be rinsed in hot clean water.

If a double sink is available, one sink can be used for washing and one for rinsing. After being washed, dishes may be placed in a rack, and the rack immersed in really hot rinsing water for about half a minute. The rack may then be lifted out of the water, and the dishes allowed to dry in the air. If dishes are dried with a cloth, the cloth must be clean. Such cloths should be washed frequently in boiling detergent solution.

Disposal of Waste

After food has been prepared and eaten waste material remains. This waste must be disposed of in a hygienic way, otherwise it may become a source of infection. House refuse, such as rotting food, may become a breeding place for flies; sugary waste attracts wasps in summer and bacteria breed in sour milk.

No solid waste material should be allowed to remain in the kitchen; it should be placed in a closed bin kept conveniently near the sink. Plastic containers with lids are suitable for this purpose. Such bins should be emptied and cleaned daily, and their contents transferred to a large bin, with a well fitting lid, kept outside. These bins should be emptied regularly, and after emptying they should be rinsed with a disinfectant solution. The area round the bin must also be kept clean.

Liquid waste may be poured down the sink, and the sink should then be rinsed with a solution of disinfectant. Milk bottles should be carefully rinsed and drained, and the inside of empty tins and jars washed out. If this is not done the food waste remaining in them is a possible source of infection.

SUMMARY

Food poisoning occurs when our bodies are invaded by large numbers of pathogenic bacteria. The Salmonella and Staphylococcus groups of bacteria both cause food poisoning, the former because the bacteria themselves cause infection and the latter by forming a poison if they are allowed to multiply in food. Thorough cooking is the best way to kill bacteria in food, though some bacteria develop heat resistant spores which can survive normal cooking. Such spores become active if food is stored in warm moist conditions, and infected food which is kept warm for a time may cause food poisoning.

The handling of food by infected people may be the cause of food poisoning. Personal hygiene is therefore most important and simple hygiene rules should be observed as a matter of routine. Hands should be washed after using the toilet, and also before handling or eating food. When coughing or sneezing the mouth and nose should be covered with a clean handkerchief. Wounds and boils should be kept covered, and clean protective clothing should be worn by food handlers.

Simple rules of hygiene should be observed at all stages in the storage, handling and preparation of food. The kitchen itself should be kept clean, as also should the equipment used in it. Cleaning is best done using a hot solution of detergent. A little disinfectant may be added to kill bacteria.

Food should be stored in a dry cool place with plenty of ventilation and with means to exclude flies and other insects. Perishable food that is to be stored for any period longer than a few hours is best kept in a refrigerator, though for periods of more than a few days a deep-freeze which freezes the food is better.

Food should be cooked thoroughly to kill any bacteria present, and then eaten at once or cooled rapidly and stored in a cool larder or refrigerator. When food has to be re-cooked, the cooking time should be long enough and the temperature high enough to ensure that the heat reaches the interior of the food.

11 Towards a World of Plenty?

If people are hungry, they need food.
If they are ill-nourished, they need good food.

Lord Boyd Orr

First of all in this chapter ask yourself one or two questions. How many meals do you have each day? How often do you feel hungry? How many different foods do you enjoy in your diet? The answer to the first question is probably that you have three main meals a day. And perhaps you've never felt *really* hungry. When you feel the first pang of hunger you can probably get hold of a sweet or eat some fruit to tide you over until the next meal. Perhaps you find the last question rather difficult to answer—you probably eat so many different foods that it is hard to work out exactly how many.

If you ask your friends the same three questions that you have just asked yourself, you will almost certainly get similar answers. But if you had been living two or three centuries ago, your answers would have been very different. You might have had to be content with one main meal a day, and there would certainly have been times when you were hungry. You might have known times when the whole country was devastated by famine. It was only just over a hundred years ago for instance that famine killed at least a million people in Ireland. And your diet would certainly have been much less varied than the one you enjoy to-day. It would have contained no tinned or frozen foods; fresh meat would have been a luxury in summer and almost unknown in winter, and fruit grown in other countries and potatoes would have been a rarity. The main items of your diet could have been counted on the fingers of your hands.

There are many reasons why our diet has improved so much in the last two hundred years. In those far off days we had to eat

Most people have a monotonous diet based on one food. Here an Indian girl eats a meal of rice, which forms the basis of the diet of most Eastern people.

the food that was grown in our own neighbourhood. To-day the improvement of transport makes it possible for us to enjoy foods from every part of the earth—tea from India and Ceylon, pineapples from Malaya, rice from Burma—the list is almost endless. Our knowledge of food preservation (see Chapter 9) is such that we are able to eat a large variety of perishable foods at any time of year. The range of food available is further increased by the addition of manufactured foods—chocolate, margarine and breakfast cereals—to mention just a few.

We must note one other important reason why our diet to-day is so much more varied than in the past. It is a very simple reason; we are much richer! During the past two hundred years our island has changed from a mainly farming country into a highly industrialized one. Our standard of living has gradually improved so that most of us are now so wealthy that we can eat as much food as we like selecting the foods we prefer—and still have enough money left over for luxuries like cars, washing machines and television sets.

Poverty and Hunger

Is the title of this chapter wrong? Are we not already living in a world of plenty? The answer to both questions is 'No'. It is just that by a lucky chance we have been born in the right place at the right time!

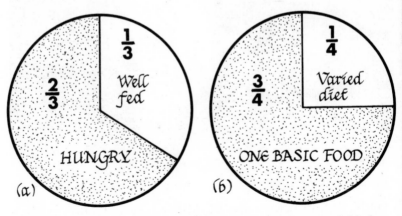

Fig. 55. (a) Two-thirds of the world population is hungry and (b) three-quarters exist on a monotonous diet of one basic food.

Most people in the world are lucky if they have one good sustaining meal a day. *Most* people in the world suffer from hunger and *most* people have a monotonous diet made up of only one basic food (see Fig. 55).

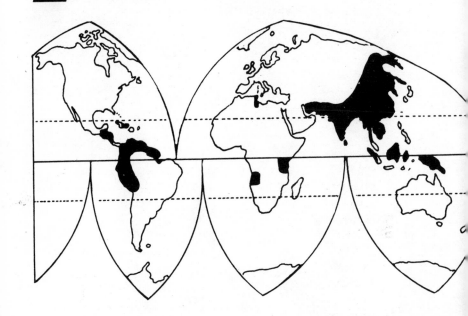

■ Regions where the daily Calorie intake is below 2,200 (the under-developed countries)

Fig. 56. Map showing the hungry regions of the world (after Dudley Stamp).

If you study the map shown in Fig. 56 you will see that most of the people of the Far East and many in parts of Africa and South America are hungry. We say that they are suffering from *under-nutrition*, meaning that they do not get enough of the essential nutrients in their diet. The minimum daily requirement of Calories for an average adult is 2,200 and so anyone receiving less than this must be hungry. As nearly two-thirds of the world population live in the 'black' areas of the map, two people out of every three must be hungry.

Unfortunately under-nutrition is not the only form of under-nourishment in the world today. In addition many people suffer from *malnutrition*. Malnutrition—meaning bad nutrition—occurs when one or more essential nutrient is absent from the diet. We have already had some examples of this. For instance in Chapter 6 we saw that someone living on a diet which lacks vitamin

The world population is going up at an increasing rate—especially in the under-developed countries where there are many more brown skins than white.

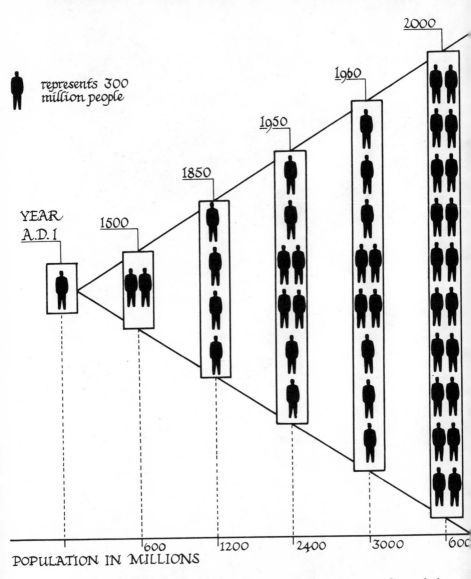

represents 300 million people

YEAR A.D. 1

1500

1850

1950

1960

2000

POPULATION IN MILLIONS

600   1200   2400   3000   600

Fig. 57. World Population Chart—showing how the rate of population growth is still increasing.

B_1 suffers from the disease *beriberi*, while lack of vitamin D causes *rickets*. Probably the most serious form of malnutrition is lack of enough protein in the diet. In parts of the world where hunger is common, as many as eight children out of ten may not have enough protein to eat, and as a result they suffer from a disease

178

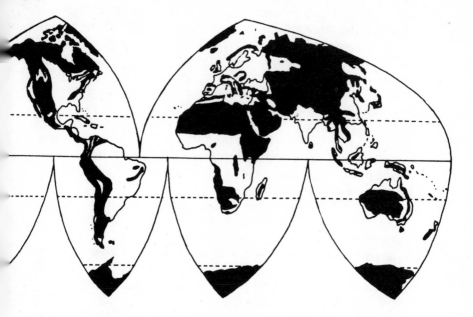

Regions which are too cold, dry or mountainous for cultivation

Fig. 58. Map showing areas of the world where it is difficult or impossible to grow food (after Dudley Stamp).

called *kwashiorkor*. It is a very unpleasant disease and even if a child survives it he may be crippled for life. We have now probably said enough to convince you that you are indeed fortunate compared to most other people—and also that the problem of hunger is one of the biggest in the world to-day.

The Challenge of Hunger

The challenge of hunger is the challenge of how to ensure that every person on the earth has a diet that will supply his needs. As most people in the developed countries already have a satisfactory diet the problem becomes one of how to feed properly the people living in the under-developed countries (Fig. 56).

The problem is getting bigger every day simply because the

number of people in the world keeps on increasing (see page 177). For every mouth there was to feed in 1850 there were two mouths to feed in 1950. This seems a very rapid increase, but the increase to-day is even greater, and for every mouth we have to feed now we shall have two in only forty or fifty years (Fig. 57). This means that to-morrow there will be about 140,000 *extra* mouths to feed compared with to-day. Somehow we must increase world food production to do two things. First, we must produce extra food for those who are hungry, and second we must produce more food for the extra mouths that are appearing at an ever increasing rate.

What a challenge! Can we possibly meet it? Well, the simple answer to that is that we *must* meet it. It is unthinkable that we can allow our fellow human beings to starve; we must use every means in our power now and in the future to overcome the challenge of starvation and hunger.

If you study the map shown in Fig. 58, you will notice that much of the land surface of the earth cannot be used for producing food. Yet even if we allow for these unproductive areas, there are still some parts of the earth left which do not as yet produce food, but which *could* produce food if properly cultivated. In fact the earth could support at least *ten* times the present population if full use was made of its resources.

At present food production is slowly increasing—but it is only increasing fast enough to feed the *increase* in population. This still leaves the problem of how to feed the hungry two-thirds of the world population. It is obvious that if we are to solve this problem we must increase food supplies by every possible means. We shall now consider how this can be done.

WAYS OF INCREASING FOOD SUPPLIES

How to get More Food from Land already under Cultivation

It is quite certain that in many parts of the under-developed regions yields of food from cultivated land can be greatly increased. For example, the yield of wheat per acre in Pakistan to-day is only one-quarter of the yield in this country. There are many ways in which such poor yields can be improved. One obvious way is to improve the quality and varieties of seed that are used. For instance, we can produce seeds that are resistant to pests, cold or drought. Increases of 50% in crop yields have been recorded by use of this simple method.

Crop yields may also be increased by the use of *chemical fertilizers*. These are now used in place of farmyard manure to put back into the soil nutrients removed by growing crops. The three main types of fertilizer are those which supply the elements nitrogen, phosphorus and potassium to the soil in forms which can be used by plants. The use of fertilizers greatly increases both the fertility of the soil and the crop yield. At present the developed regions use seven times as much fertilizer per acre of cultivated land as the under-developed countries. From this you can see that we can hope to improve greatly crop yields in the undeveloped countries by using more fertilizers.

Left: The Tractor is replacing the ox (Mexico).

Below: One way of increasing food production is by intensive farming of animals such as poultry.

In many under-developed countries the farms are still using the primitive tools that have been used for centuries. By using modern tools and by replacing animal-drawn equipment by mechanized equipment, the efficiency of food production can be greatly increased. In this country the horse has been replaced by the tractor, and in many countries the pace of agriculture is still geared to the slow plodding steps of ox or bullock. When you think that one modern combine harvesting machine can do the work of forty men you will see the great advantages of mechanizing farm equipment (see page 180).

Irrigation

A great deal of land, at present unfertile, could be used for growing food if only it could be supplied with regular amounts of water. Even desert land could be brought into use if water was available. This problem is being tackled in many ways, one of the most important of which is *irrigation*. Natural water supplies are conserved by storing them in huge man-made reservoirs. The stored water may then be used to irrigate the surrounding lands in times of drought. For example, a great dam has been built at Kariba, between Northern and Southern Rhodesia, which will store water from the Zambesi river, and make it possible to irrigate millions of acres of unused land.

Food from the Sea

When you think of farming you probably think of the growing of crops or the breeding of animals on the earth's land surface. But it is also possible to farm the sea, and there is far more sea available than land on the surface of the earth. At present only about 1% of our food is fish, but the sea could make a much bigger contribution to our diet if we cultivated it properly. Indeed it is believed that we could more than double the present world fish catch, without over-fishing the sea and inland waters.

There are many ways of increasing fish catches, especially in the under-developed countries where such increases are most urgently needed. Methods of fishing in some countries are still very primitive. The boats that are used often have no engine and so fishing

is at the mercy of the tides and winds. Some boats are no more than rafts with sails, and so can only put to sea in good weather and for short periods. When good sturdy sea-going boats with engines replace the sailing boats and when good nets and equipment are used, yields of fish rapidly improve (see below).

In developed countries new types of fishing vessels—you might call them fish factories—are replacing the old. These newer ships can stay at sea for months at a time and can preserve the fish as they are caught.

There are also great possibilities of getting more fish from inland waters. Such waters can be farmed in the same way as the land by breeding fish just as we breed animals.

Fishing boats in Ceylon fitted with outboard engines are rapidly improving fish catches. Only a few years ago there were no fishing boats with engines in Ceylon.

Food that gets Lost

It is sad to think that one-fifth of the food that should be gathered in from crops planted by man, never reaches us. It is lost in the sense that it is destroyed or damaged by disease, insects and other pests. One of the most terrifying insect pests is the locust. A locust has a huge appetite and eats its own weight of food every day. Great swarms of locusts may contain a thousand million insects, and such swarms advance over the earth, eating all the growing crops as they go. Such swarms have been the dread of farmers ever since biblical times, and even now they are a menace in Africa and other countries (see below).

It is obvious that if we can control and get rid of locusts and other insect pests we shall greatly increase food supplies. Chemists have made many chemicals which kill insects; they are called *insecticides*. Other chemical substances have been made that will fight diseases in both plants and animals. These chemical substances make it possible to wage continual war against pests and diseases. They can often be sprayed onto large areas of crops by aircraft. This method has even been used to spray and kill locust swarms in flight. Cattle can often be protected from disease by means of vaccination.

Locust swarms are still a menace in Africa and other countries.

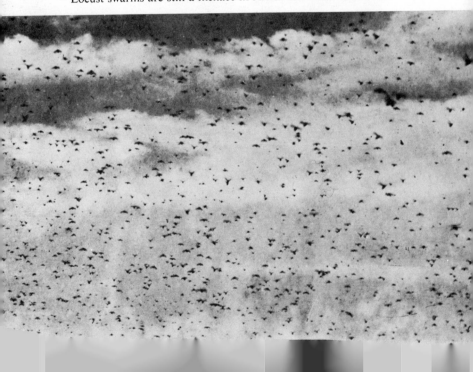

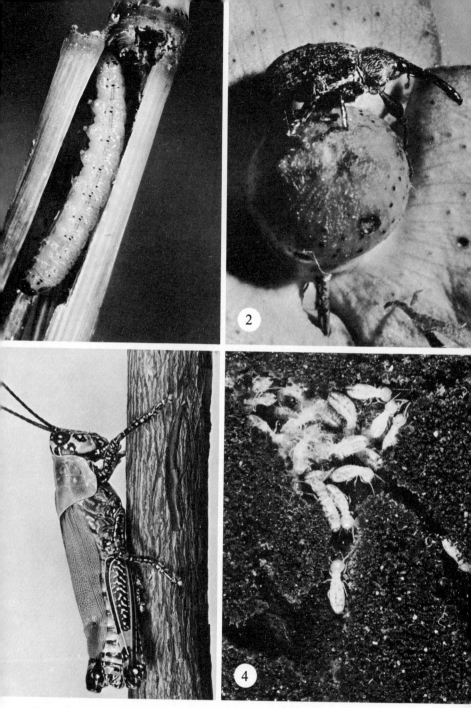

Pests destroy growing crops.   (1) Larva of rice stem borer.   (2) Cotton weevil on cotton boll.   (3) Grasshopper.   (4) Termites.

Even if crops are safely harvested, there is still a danger that they may never reach us. As soon as cereals are stored they are attacked by both insects and rats. Up to 10% of the world's supply of grain is destroyed in this way—enough to feed one person in ten all the year round. Modern methods of storage and treatment of the crops are being developed to cut down these losses.

New Sources of Food

We have already discussed several ways of increasing food supplies—there are many others we have not had space to consider. Better transportation, better methods of preservation, better understanding of the principles of nutrition—all these, and many more, can increase the amount of food available to us. In addition there are other exciting possibilities for increasing food supplies.

Only a few years ago travel meant moving around the earth by land or sea. Now it includes air travel, and already we are looking forward to the future when it will include travel to the moon, and perhaps other planets. So it is with food. In the past diet was restricted to food that could be grown near the home. Now we can use foods from many countries and thus enjoy a varied diet. In the future, we shall be able to make use of new foods grown in new ways.

For example, although the amount of land available for farming is limited, the amount of salt and fresh water available is enormous. But, you will say, can we grow crops in salt and fresh water? The answer is simple—yes. Certain plants living in fresh water are able to use the water and, with the help of carbon dioxide and sunlight, build up carbohydrate. If the water contains suitable nutrients they also build up protein. A minute green plant called *chlorella* is able to perform these wonders.

A single chlorella plant is so small that to see it you would have to look through a microscope. If it is so small, you may think that it is not much use as a food, but new plants form so rapidly that in only 12 hours its weight increases fourfold. In ideal conditions over 100 tons of chlorella should be obtained from one acre in a year. Chlorella is so rich in protein and its yield is so great that—in theory at any rate—an area of only about three square miles would be needed to supply enough protein for all the people

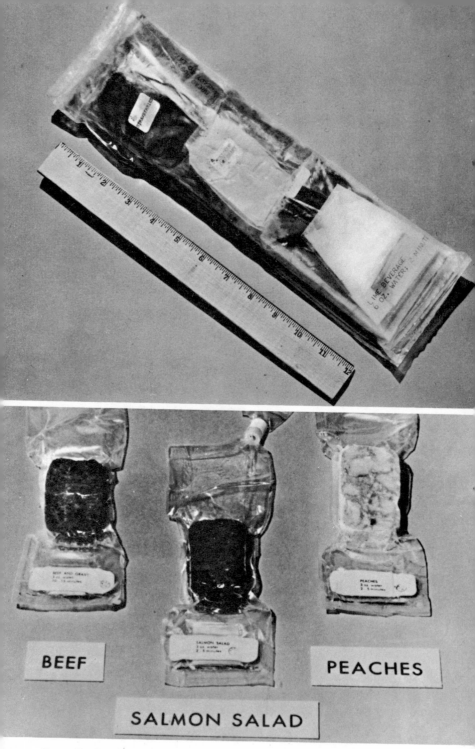

BEEF

SALMON SALAD

PEACHES

Space Food. Complete meals are being developed for use in spacecraft. Note that the food has been dried to make it compact, and that envelopes containing water to rehydrate the food are included.

in Britain! At present farming on water is only in the trial stage, but in the future chlorélla may be as common as cabbage is to-day!

One of the main causes of malnutrition in the world is shortage of protein. In searching for new sources of food we shall, therefore, be especially on the lookout for new sources of protein. We obtain much of our protein food indirectly by growing plants, which are mainly carbohydrate, and feeding the plants to animals. Eventually we eat the animals which supply us with valuable animal protein (see page 68). Unfortunately this is not a profitable method of producing protein because we only get back about one tenth of the protein that we fed to the animal!

It would clearly be much simpler and more profitable if we could extract the protein from the plants directly without getting

Soya beans provide one new source of protein; the beans are ground into a protein-rich flour and this is spun into fibres (shown in the photograph) which have some slight resemblance to meat fibres. Colourings and flavourings are added to the fibres which are then shaped to resemble meat (see next page).

an animal to do this for us.   Many plant materials, such as grass, cannot be eaten by us directly, because they are mostly cellulose and so indigestible.   However, we can extract the protein from such plants and so make a highly nutritious protein food.   At present we waste many millions of tons of plant material every year, so that in the future we may obtain large amounts of concentrated protein food from such sources.

We can also hope to obtain protein from non-plant protein materials which at present are wasted.   When vegetable oils are extracted from groundnuts, coconuts and the like, a valuable but indigestible protein-rich residue remains.   This is often used as cattle food or fertilizer, but if processed to remove the indigestible part it could be converted into a valuable protein food.   In a similar way we can produce a highly nutritious protein-rich flour from whole fish.

Finally, some micro-organisms are able to grow, multiply and build up protein very quickly starting from sugar and various

This delicious-looking 'meat' is in fact a meatless 'steak' made from soya beans.   Such vegetable protein foods are now being made commercially in America.

mineral elements.   Certain yeasts are able to do this, and in the future yeast cultivation should be able to supply us with useful amounts of protein.   Perhaps one day we shall grow yeast instead of rearing cattle, for whereas half a ton of bullock only produces one pound of protein in 24 hours, half a ton of yeast can produce *fifty* tons of protein in the same time!

Putting Theory into Practice

We have seen that there are many ways in which we can increase food supplies *now*; also that there are many ways in which we can develop new methods in the *future*.   But in order to overcome world hunger we must tackle the problem on a world scale. This needs a world-wide organization to carry out the work and luckily we have such an organization in the *United Nations*.   A special agency of the United Nations looks after world food problems.   It is called the *Food and Agriculture Organization* (F.A.O.).   In 1960 F.A.O. launched a special campaign to overcome hunger in the world—the *Freedom from Hunger Campaign*.

One of the objects of the Freedom from Hunger Campaign was to make everyone aware of the problems of hunger and starvation. For one thing is quite certain, the problem of hunger is so great that it can only be solved if we use *every* method available to us. To do this every one of us has his or her part to play.   It surely cannot be right that you and I have more than enough to eat while most other people in the world are hungry.   We can help to solve the problem by understanding what the problem is and how it can be solved, also by explaining it to our friends and finally by using food wisely ourselves.   Much of this book has been about good nutrition and there are many ways in which we can use our new knowledge about food and nutrition to improve our own diet— and also the diet of others.

We *can* solve the problem of hunger because we have the means to do it.   We *shall* solve the problem if we have the *will* to do it.

SUMMARY

In past centuries our diet in this country was restricted to foods which could be grown around our homes.   Now we enjoy a much more varied diet containing foods from many countries; we also

have plenty to eat. Most people in the world, however, are less fortunate than us, and they do not have enough to eat. Many suffer from under-nutrition and malnutrition. The problem of feeding the hungry is made more difficult because the world population is getting bigger at an increasing rate.

In order to feed everyone properly food supplies must be increased and methods of distributing food must be improved. We can increase food supplies from land already being cultivated by improving the quality of seeds, by using increased amounts of chemical fertilizers and by mechanising farm equipment. We can also make desert lands fertile by irrigation.

We can hope to double fish supplies from the sea by mechanising fishing boats and improving equipment. We can also obtain more fish from inland waters by careful fish cultivation. Food supplies can be increased if we can control pests and diseases that attack plants and animals. Insecticides and other chemicals are now available which will do this.

In the near future we may hope to increase food supplies by making use of new foods grown in new ways. For example, we may be able to farm inland waters by growing plants, such as chlorella, in them. Protein is the nutrient in shortest supply, and we hope to increase supplies of protein by extracting protein from plant and other vegetable materials that are at present wasted. Protein supplies may also be increased by cultivating yeasts, which build up protein very quickly from readily available starting materials.

The problem of world hunger is so large that is can only be solved by efforts on a world-wide scale. The Food and Agriculture Organization of the United Nations is at present trying to help solve world food problems.

Suggestions for Further Reading

CHAPTERS 1, 2 AND 3

The Chemicals of Life, *I. Asimov*, 1957, Bell. A simple account of enzymes, vitamins, proteins and digestion among other things.
The Living River, *I. Asimov*, 1959, Abelard-Schuman. The story of the bloodstream, including an account of what happens to nutrients in the body.
Molecules To-day and To-morrow, *M. O. Hyde*, 1964, Harrap.

CHAPTER 4

The Potato as a Food, *G. M. Chappell*, Potato Marketing Board.
The Story of Margarine, *M. Blackmore*, 2nd ed., 1960, Unilever Educational Booklet.
Sugar, 1964, Free booklet, Tate and Lyle Ltd.
Vegetable Oils and Fats, *G. Edwards*, revised ed., 1968, Unilever Educational Booklet.

CHAPTER 5

Cheesemaking, 4th ed., 1959, H.M.S.O.
Sea Harvest, *N. Holland*, 2nd ed., 1959, Unilever Educational Booklet.

CHAPTER 6

The Story of Tea, Brooke Bond Tea Ltd.
The Tree of the Golden Pod (story of cocoa), *H. J. Deverson*, A Bournville publication.

CHAPTER 7

Manual of Nutrition, 6th ed., 1961, reprinted 1966, H.M.S.O.
Planning Meals, *F. le Gros Clark and E. M. Gage*, 1960, reprinted 1963, Methuen.

CHAPTER 8

ABC of Cookery, 6th ed., 1962, reprinted 1966, H.M.S.O.
Better Cookery, *A. King*, revised ed., 1962, reprinted 1965, Mills and Boon.
Cookery for Schools, *M. M. Neal*, 1961, reprinted 1966, Blackie.
Learning to Cook, *M. Foster*, 1966, reprinted 1967, Heinemann.

CHAPTER 9

ABC of Preserving, 4th ed., 1960, reprinted 1964, H.M.S.O.
Domestic Preservation of Fruit and Vegetables, 11th ed., 1966, H.M.S.O.
Quick-frozen Foods, *R. Sinclair*, revised ed., 1961, Unilever Educational Booklet.

CHAPTER 10

Hygiene for Nursing Students, *A. E. Pavey*, 8th ed., 1958, Faber and Faber.

CHAPTER 11

Feeding the World, special issue of *Science Journal*, May 1968.
Food for Man, *W. R. Aykroyd*, 1964, Pergamon.
The Hungry World, *E. Stamp*, 1967, E. J. Arnold.

For more Advanced Reading

A Chemical Approach to Food and Nutrition, *B. A. Fox and A. G. Cameron*, 1961, reprinted 1968, University of London Press.
Food Science and Technology, *M. Pyke*, 1964, Murray.

Revision Questions

The author and publishers are grateful to the following examining bodies for their kind permission to reprint questions from past examination papers. With the exception of questions from City and Guilds papers, all those quoted are from General Certificate of Education ordinary level papers. The abbreviations given below are those used in the questions that follow.

Oxford and Cambridge Schools Examination Board, Domestic Subjects	(O. & C.)
Northern Universities Joint Matriculation Board, Domestic Subjects:	
syllabus A	(J.M.B.A.)
syllabus C	(J.M.B.C.)
University of London, Domestic Subjects:	
Cookery	(U.O.L.)
City and Guilds of London Institute:	
Catering Trades Basic Training Course (150)	(C. & G. 150)
Domestic Cookery (243)	(C. & G. 243)
Advanced Domestic Cookery (244)	(C. & G. 244)

Chapter 1

1. What are nutrients? Name the different types of nutrient and explain the purpose of each.
2. Why are tea, coffee and pepper not classed as foods while sugar and salt are?
3. Explain the terms element, atom and molecule and give two examples of each.
4. Why is it that we call sodium chloride a food, but the elements of which it is made—sodium and chlorine—poisons?

Chapter 2

1. Explain the difference in structure and properties of a monosaccharide, a disaccharide and a polysaccharide and give one example of each.
2. What is *hydrolysis*? How would you hydrolyse sucrose and starch and what would the end products be in each case?
3. What is inversion and what is its importance in (a) the making of honey by bees and (b) the making of jam?
4. Explain briefly how proteins are built up from amino acids and explain what happens when a simple protein such as ovalbumin is heated gently.

5. From what four units is a fat molecule built? Why are some fats solid and some liquid at normal air temperatures?

Chapter 3

1. What is digestion? Explain briefly what happens to proteins, fats and carbohydrates during digestion.
2. What is an enzyme? Explain the importance of enzymes in the digestion of proteins.
3. How do saliva, hydrochloric acid and water assist the process of digestion of food?
4. The following menu is typical of a mid-day meal during the winter months: brown stew, carrots, potatoes, apple pie and custard. Name the various food constituents present in this meal and give an account of the digestion of three of these.   (J.M.B.C.)
5. Explain, with the aid of diagrams, the changes that take place during the digestion and absorption of a poached egg on buttered toast.   (J.M.B.A.)
6. Why is it necessary to include foods containing roughage in the daily diet? Name *three* different types of food which contain roughage, giving specific examples in each case. Plan meals for a day for a schoolgirl of your own age. Indicate the building and protective foods provided by each meal.   (O. & C.)
7. How are waste and useless materials removed from the body? Describe *one* method in detail. What rules of health and hygiene should be followed to ensure the proper functioning of the excretory system?   (J.M.B.A.)
8. Describe in detail the organs of the digestive tract. Make a diagram to illustrate your answer. What do you know of: (a) amino acids; (b) metabolism?   (C. & G. 244)
9. Describe the small intestine and give in detail the processes of digestion that take place there.   (C. & G. 244)

Chapter 4

1. Why does the body need energy and how does food supply it?
2. From what foods do we obtain energy? How do we use up the energy gained? What difference would you make between the diet for a manual worker and the diet for an office worker? Give examples to show the difference.
3. With the aid of a diagram explain how wholemeal flour differs from ordinary white flour. Give the recipe for making a wholemeal loaf using yeast. Explain the action which takes place when making the bread.   (O. & C.)
4. (a) Classify, with examples, the various types of grain used in making milk puddings.

(b) How much grain is needed to make (i) a pint milk pudding, (ii) a pint milk mould?

Give the recipe and instructions for making a grain milk pudding in which an egg is used. (O. & C.)

5. State the general composition of the wheat grain. What property makes it suitable for use in bread and cake mixtures? What is the nutritive value of (a) semolina, (b) wholemeal bread, (c) white bread? Give instructions for the day-to-day storage of bread in the home. (J.M.B.A.)

6. Why is it necessary to include in the diet (a) fresh fruit and vegetables, (b) some form of fat? Discuss the relative merits, in the diet, of butter and margarine. (J.M.B.A.)

7. Name *three* raising agents used in cookery, giving for each one examples of its use. Explain in detail the changes that take place during the preparation and baking of (a) a loaf of bread, (b) Yorkshire pudding. (J.M.B.A.)

8. Name the fats and oils used in the preparation and cooking of food. In each case, state the purpose for which they are used. (C. & G. 150)

9. What is the value of yeast in the diet? State what changes take place during the making and baking of bread. (C. & G. 150)

Chapter 5

1. Show by your knowledge of the nature of protein how foods containing protein build the body and why some of the foods have more value than others. Compare the adult's need for protein with that of the child. (J.M.B.A.)

2. 'The body contains nineteen or so major inorganic mineral substances, all of which must be derived from food.' These substances are used for three main purposes. What are these purposes? Give an account of the part calcium and phosphorus play in the diet. (J.M.B.A.)

3. Give the food value of eggs. What precautions should you take in (a) the preparation of mayonnaise, (b) the preparation and cooking of scrambled eggs? (C. & G. 150)

4. What is the food value of eggs? Besides being a valuable food what other advantages have eggs in cookery? Give clear instructions for making a breakfast dish using two eggs. (U.O.L.)

5. What is the nutritive value of eggs? In what respects do they fail to be a perfect food? How can these deficiencies be overcome? Giving one example in each case, enumerate the ways in which eggs may be used in cookery. (J.M.B.A.)

6. Compare the food values of cheese and eggs. Suggest interesting ways that each might be used as a main dish in a meal for vegetarians. Describe the making of one dish in detail. (C. & G. 244)

7. Explain why cheese is such a valuable food. In what ways can cheese be introduced into the diet? Give instructions for making one cooked cheese dish. (U.O.L.)
8. Name and describe *three* different varieties of cheese. Give the composition of cheese and the effect of cooking on its food value. Suggest a cheese dish suitable for the main course for high tea during the winter months. List and calculate the cost of the ingredients used. (J.M.B.A.)
9. Why is milk considered an important item in the diet? Account for the differences in the diet of a three-month-old baby and a one-year-old child. Give the proportions of ingredients that should be used to make up a pint of milk for: (i) a rice pudding; (ii) a chocolate mould; (iii) a baked egg custard. (O. & C.)
10. What is the food value of milk? What may cause its deterioration? How would you ensure that milk was kept fresh in summer if you had no refrigerator. Why is milk of such importance in all households? (C. & G. 243)
11. Describe the structure of lean meat. How is meat affected by moist and dry heat? Give instructions for making a meat stew.
(U.O.L.)
12. How can fish be classified? Give two examples of fish in each class. Compare the classes of fish as regards: (a) food value; (b) digestibility. What advice would you give to an inexperienced cook about choosing fish? (U.O.L.)
13. What is the value of fish in the diet? Suggest a suitable fish dish for (a) breakfast, (b) a birthday luncheon party, (c) supper. In each case give the other dishes included to complete the meal and explain how the meal is balanced. (J.M.B.A.)
14. What is the value of fish in the diet? Mention *three* different methods of cooking fish. Using diagrams and notes show how (a) to fillet flat fish, (b) to bone herrings. (J.M.B.C.)

Chapter 6

1. What is the value of protective foods in the diet? Give the menus for a day's meals for a teenager—breakfast, mid-day meal and supper—showing how you would use protective foods.

(C. & G. 150)
2. Explain the term 'protective' as applied to foods. Giving reasons and examples, state which you consider to be the essential protective foods in the diet of a teenager. Plan *two* consecutive days' menus for a schoolgirl, indicating the building and protective foods present. (O. & C.)
3. What are vitamins? Write a short account of four important vitamins. What precautions should be taken to prevent loss of vitamins from food? (U.O.L.)

4. What are the various vitamins and in what foods are they found? What effect would (a) a slight lack and (b) a prolonged deficiency of each vitamin have on a person? (C. & G. 244)
5. Give the names, sources and functions of any *five* mineral constituents in the diet. (J.M.B.A.)
6. 'Vegetables are an essential part of a well balanced diet.' Discuss this statement. With what other ingredients would you combine each of the following to prepare an appetizing supper dish: (a) vegetable marrow; (b) spinach; (c) cauliflower; (d) tomatoes? Give reasons for your choice. (J.M.B.A.)
7. What is the value of vegetables in the diet? Classify vegetables, giving examples. What steps should be taken to ensure the vegetables are not spoilt during preparation, cooking and serving? (C. & G. 243)
8. Why are vegetables and fruit so essential in the diet? Give what you consider to be a good selection. (C. & G. 150)
9. Why are vegetables necessary in the diet? What is meant by the conservative method of cooking? Give clear instructions for cooking conservatively: (a) carrots; (b) potatoes; (c) cabbage. (U.O.L.)
10. Why is it important to include fresh vegetables and fruit in the diet? Give *three* attractive ways of serving each of the following: (a) potatoes; (b) tomatoes; (c) celery. Give the nutritive value of each dish. (J.M.B.C.)

Chapter 7
1. Explain what is meant by *a balanced diet*. In what ways can the housewife ensure that the family eat and enjoy well balanced meals? (J.M.B.C.)
2. What is a well balanced meal? Give two balanced lunch menus; one suitable for (a) a manual worker, (b) an adolescent. (C. & G. 150)
3. What precautions should be taken when preparing packed meals to ensure that they are well balanced? Give the contents of a suitable packed mid-day meal for: (a) a manual worker in winter; (b) a school-girl in summer. Give some useful points to bear in mind when making sandwiches. (U.O.L.)
4. What are the main points to remember when compiling menus? Write out (a) a three-course lunch menu suitable for women executives, (b) a five-course dinner menu suitable for a special occasion. Give appropriate wines that might be served with each meal. (C. & G. 244)
5. State the points to be considered when planning diets for invalids. Plan the menu for two days for a girl, aged sixteen, who is recovering from an attack of mumps; give reasons for the choice made. (J.M.B.A.)

6. What points must the housewife consider when planning meals for the family? Plan meals for Saturday and Sunday for a family of two adults and twin girls, aged fourteen. State briefly the reasons for the choice of dishes. (J.M.B.A.)

7. What should be the chief considerations in planning meals for (a) children under five years of age, (b) a bed-ridden elderly person? (J.M.B.A.)

8. A great many people go out for the day, either for work or pleasure, taking packed meals with them. What are the main points to remember when arranging packed meals? Keeping in mind the points you have given, suggest two packed meals, one suitable for winter, and one for summer and state how these meals would be packed and carried. (C. & G. 243)

9. What are vegetarians? From what foods do they get their supply of protein? Give the menus for one day for a vegetarian family. (C. & G. 243)

10. How do you ensure well balanced meals for vegetarians? Plan a two-course evening meal for each night for a week for two vegetarians who have a packed lunch. (U.O.L.)

11. Those who plan meals, cook and otherwise handle food have a tremendous responsibility. Discuss the main points which they should consider. (C. & G. 243)

12. What is the importance of raw food in the diet? Give the menus for a mid-day meal in summer and a mid-day meal in winter in which raw food is included. (C. & G. 243)

Chapter 8

1. Good cookery is 'an art, a craft, and a science'. Discuss this in relation to the work you have been doing, giving examples to illustrate your points. (O. & C.)

2. Draw a labelled diagram to show the structure of a thermometer. State, with reasons, the oven temperatures suitable for cooking each of the following: (a) bread; (b) a baked custard; (c) a brown stew; (d) a rich fruit Christmas cake; (e) sausage rolls (using flaky pastry). (J.M.B.A.)

3. How is heat transferred during the following cooking processes: (a) grilling steak; (b) making egg custard sauce in a double cooker; (c) baking Yorkshire pudding? What action has the heat on the main food constituents in each case? (J.M.B.C.)

4. Name and define *five* different methods of cooking. Plan a well balanced main meal using only one method of cooking. (U.O.L.)

5. State the advantages of steaming as a method of cooking. Give three different methods of steaming food and illustrate your answer with diagrams. Plan a dinner cooked mainly by steaming. (U.O.L.)

6. Compare stewing and roasting as methods of cooking beef. Give the cuts of beef that could be used in each case. How would you ensure success when making a brown stew? (C. & G. 243)

7. Discuss the value of boiling as a method of cooking. What joints of meat are best suited to boiling? Describe the preparation and cooking of a joint which is to be boiled. Suggest suitable accompaniments to serve with this joint for a dinner. (J.M.B.C.)

8. Why is it customary to cook meat? Name the chief cuts of lamb or mutton and state, giving reasons, a suitable method of cooking each cut which you have named. (J.M.B.A.)

9. Explain carefully the changes which take place when (a) a chop is grilled, (b) milk curdles, (c) yeast rolls are baked. (C. & G. 243)

10. What is the object of coating food which is to be fried? Name *three* coatings and give *one* example of the use of each. Describe in detail the preparation, frying and serving of *one* dish mentioned. Explain how to deal with a pan of shallow fat that is on fire.
    (J.M.B.A.)

11. There is now a variety of fats from which to choose for cooking purposes. Which fats are suitable and practical for the following processes: (a) making short crust pastry; (b) deep-fat frying; (c) making a rich cake mixture? Give the reasons for the fats chosen. Write notes on the care of fat for deep frying. (J.M.B.C.)

12. Write an account of frying as a method of cooking. (U.O.L.)

13. What is the difference in food value of fresh, canned, dried and frozen peas? Explain in detail how you would cook frozen peas to give the best nutritive value and results. (C. & G. 150)

14. Explain fully the action of the following: (a) yeast in breadmaking; (b) baking powder in cakes; (c) hot fat on egg and crumb coated food. (C. & G. 243)

15. What is the principle underlying the cooking of eggs? State in detail how you would prepare, cook and serve (a) a poached egg and (b) a baked egg custard. (C. & G. 243)

16. What is the food value of an egg? Describe the different ways in which eggs may be used in cookery, giving examples and any special care required. (C. & G. 244)

17. What special care is required when cooking egg custards? Give the recipe and method of making (a) an egg custard sauce, (b) a baked egg custard. (C. & G. 243)

18. What governs the quantity of baking powder used in cake making? What happens to a plain cake mixture when (a) excess baking powder is used, (b) insufficient baking powder is used? (J.M.B.C.)

19. What is the action of yeast as a raising agent? Give an explanation of each process necessary during the preparation and baking of yeast mixtures. (C. & G. 244)

20. In what way does self-raising flour differ from plain flour? What are the advantages and disadvantages in the use of self-raising flour? For what purposes is it essential to use *plain* flour? How should flour be stored? (U.O.L.)
21. What methods are used in cooking for making mixtures light? Explain in detail the changes which take place in two cases.
(U.O.L.)

Chapter 9

1. Explain the terms (a) chemical preservation, (b) dehydration, (c) pasteurization and (d) sterilization. Explain how milk is pasteurized and explain also the advantages of pasteurization.
2. Describe how refrigeration can be used to preserve food. What conditions would you use to preserve the following by refrigeration (a) milk for a day; (b) lettuce for a week; (c) frozen peas for a month?
3. What do you understand by preservation? List the various ways of preserving food. Give details for carrying out one method of preserving fruit. (U.O.L.)
4. What general principle underlies all methods of preserving foods? Give *six* different methods of preserving foods and show how each method is an example of this principle. (J.M.B.A.)
5. Name *four* methods of preserving food, giving examples in each case. Describe the carrying out of *one* of these methods. (U.O.L.)
6. On what foods and under what conditions are moulds most likely to form? Give reasons for your statements. What steps can be taken to prevent the growth of moulds?
7. What is the importance of vegetables in the diet? Assess the relative merits of fresh, frozen, canned and dried vegetables.
(C. & G. 243)
8. What are the principles which underlie the preservation of fruit by jam making? Give a recipe and clear instructions for making 3 lb. of fruit into jam. How should this be stored? (U.O.L.)

Chapter 10

1. As a food handler, how would you personally make sure that your standard of hygiene was beyond reproach? (C. & G. 150)
2. What do you consider to be the importance of uniform in the catering trade? What should the particular uniform mean personally to (a) a chambermaid, and (b) a waiter or chef? (C. & G. 150)
3. What safeguards can be taken by the housewife in the storage and preparation of food in order to avoid the spread of infection in the family? (U.O.L.)
4. What are the causes of deterioration of foods and how dangerous is this deterioration to health? Link up your knowledge of the

causes of food deterioration with the general rules to be observed when keeping foodstuffs fresh. (C. & G. 244)

5. What causes contamination of food? What steps would you take to prevent such contamination? (C. & G. 150)

6. How would you organise your own washing up to make sure that it is carried out according to the best standards of hygiene so that everything is fit for future use? (C. & G. 150)

7. What steps would you take to ensure that the principles of good hygiene are carried out in your own kitchen? (C. & G. 244)

8. It was found, when enquiring into a case of food poisoning in a catering establishment that the cotton piping bags and other apparatus were washed in a sink of luke warm water. What is wrong with this method? How would you deal with such apparatus? (C. & G. 150)

9. Why are flies dangerous when in contact with food? Describe measures which should be taken to prevent food from becoming contaminated by flies. Describe how to (a) dispose of waste matter from the kitchen, (b) take care of the dustbin. (J.M.B.A.)

10. There is an epidemic of food poisoning in your village. Describe what steps would be taken by you to safeguard your family.
(O. & C.)

11. What are the general rules to be observed in personal hygiene? Explain the importance of (a) fresh air, (b) sleep, (c) exercise, when caring for a toddler. (O. & C.)

12. For reasons of economy it is sometimes necessary to reheat food. State the points to remember in order to make reheated foods into palatable and digestible meals. Plan three well-balanced mid-day meals, in each case making use of some left-over food in the main dish. (U.O.L.)

13. What are the essential features of a good storecupboard for dry goods? Give rules for the care and cleaning of the storecupboard and its contents. (U.O.L.)

14. What are the essentials of a good larder? Describe how a larder should be used and maintained in order to keep food fresh, and to avoid waste. (U.O.L.)

15. 'A refrigerator is essential in a small modern house.' Discuss this statement. Describe how the maximum use may be made of the storage space in a refrigerator. How should it be kept in good working order? (J.M.B.A.)

16. Draw a diagram of a small domestic refrigerator indicating the storage places for different foods. Give rules with reasons for the use of the refrigerator. (U.O.L.)

Chapter 11

1. What is malnutrition? Describe three diseases that are caused by

malnutrition, and explain what causes them and how they could be prevented.
2. Many people alive to-day are hungry. Discuss this statement, explaining why so many people go hungry and which parts of the world have the greatest hunger problems.
3. Explain how the following can increase food supplies; (a) chemical fertilizers; (b) irrigation; (c) insecticides.
4. Write a short account of how new sources of food from both land and water may be used in the future to increase food supplies.
5. What part can you play in helping to meet the 'challenge of hunger'?
6. How is the United Nations meeting the 'challenge of hunger'?

General questions

1. Write notes on *four* of the following: (a) custard powder; (b) coffee; (c) vanilla; (d) margarine; (e) raisins; (f) demerara sugar. (U.O.L.)
2. Give reasons for:
   (a) Feeling sleepy after a large dinner.
   (b) Fried fish breaking up during cooking.
   (c) Watery scrambled eggs.
   (d) Jam which has not set.
   (e) A large cake which has risen to a peak.   (O. & C.)
3. Give a simple scientific explanation of each of the following:
   (a) Water in an open pan boils away more quickly than in a pan with a lid.
   (b) The handles of some pans get unbearably hot whilst others remain cool.
   (c) Food in a refrigerator should be covered.
   (d) The contents of a deep fat pan appear to boil at one stage when the pan is being heated.
   (e) A scald from steam may be more serious than one from boiling water.   (J.M.B.A.)
4 Write notes on *four* of the following: (a) gluten; (b) panada; (c) cornflour; (d) yeast; (e) prunes.   (U.O.L.)
5. (a) Why are some joints of meat much cheaper than others? Name *two* cheap cuts of beef and *two* of lamb, saying how you would cook each.
   (b) Where are the salivary glands situated, and what is their function? What other glands take part in the digestive process?
                                                              (O. & C.)
6. Write notes on the following: (a) gelatine; (b) oatmeal; (c) bouquet garni; (d) bicarbonate of soda; (e) cottage cheese.   (U.O.L.)
7. Compare the nutritive value of: (a) wholemeal and white bread;

(b) thick and clear soups; (c) oily and white fish; (d) margarine
and butter.
(U.O.L.)

8. What are the essentials of a good soup and why should soup-making
be encouraged? Give a recipe and method of making a thick
soup.
(U.O.L.)

9. What are the important nutritive values of the following foods: (a)
cheese; (b) liver; (c) milk; (d) watercress? Give ways in which
any *two* of these foods may be included in the diet. (J.M.B.C.)

10. Write a paragraph on any *four* of the following topics:

(a) The essential qualities of a good soup.
(b) The different types of flour used in cookery.
(c) Convalescent cookery.
(d) Varieties of coatings for fried foods.
(e) The importance of personal and kitchen hygiene in the preven-
tion of food contamination. (O. & C.)

11. Explain the changes that take place when:
(a) Baking powder is used as a raising agent in a cake mixture.
(b) Milk turns sour. (U.O.L.)

Index